THE
MARLINSPIKE
SAILOR

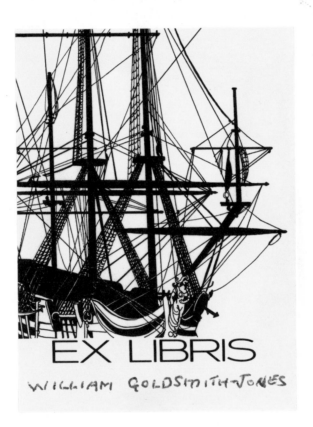

EX LIBRIS

Other books by Hervey Garrett Smith:

Arts of the Sailor
Boat Carpentry
How to Choose a Sailboat
Racing Sailor's Bible
Small Boat Sailors Bible

THE
MARLINSPIKE SAILOR

By HERVEY GARRETT SMITH

International Marine
Camden, Maine

Published by International Marine®, an imprint of McGraw-Hill, Inc.

20 19 18 17 16 15 14 13 12 11

Library of Congress Cataloging-in-Publication-Data
Smith, Hervey Garrett.
    The marlinspike sailor / by Hervey Garrett Smith.
        p. cm.
    Originally published: Tuckahoe, N.Y. : J. De Graff, 1971.
    Includes index.
    ISBN 0-07-059218-7 (alk. paper)
    1. Marline spike seamanship. I. Title.
VM531.S573 1993
623.88'82—dc20   93-25448
                                              CIP

Questions regarding the content of this book should be addressed to:
International Marine
P.O. Box 220
Camden, ME 04843

This book is printed on acid-free paper.

Printed by Malloy Litho, Ann Arbor, Michigan

Foreword

HERVEY GARRETT SMITH, the author of this book, is a seaman in the finest sense of the word. He has sailed boats all his life. He also has designed and built them. In addition he is an artist, and the quality of his work is proclaimed by his superb drawings which, when they were first published in The Rudder magazine, drew enthusiastic acclaim.

The author is imbued with the history of seafaring. He constantly searches for the best, and works toward keeping it alive and passing it on to the yachtsmen of today and tomorrow, the true inheritors of the traditions of the old days, when the world's transportation at sea depended on wind driven vessels.

Knowledge of marlinspike seamanship is what distinguishes the true seaman from the man who merely ventures upon the water at infrequent intervals. No one can become a skipper, or should aspire to the distinction, who has not mastered knots, palm and needle work, and the making of small objects on board as necessary. In fact the few required knots, hitches or bends should be so well known that they can be tied blindfolded or in the dark. The rank of able seaman must be earned.

The greatest single value of the author's work is the amazing clarity he achieves with his drawings. He has set a new standard for all time. Rope is a difficult subject to draw. Like the sea itself it changes its appearance constantly.

BORIS LAUER-LEONARDI

Introduction

Since this book was first published some twenty years ago, the boating industry has been completely revolutionized, through chemistry.

Man-made synthetic filaments have supplanted natural fibers in the manufacture of cordage, and the tarred hemp rope used by sailors for a thousand years has suddenly become obsolete.

Cotton duck, which alternately shrank, stretched, mildewed and rotted, has been replaced by completely stable synthetic sailcloth whose performance can be anticipated and controlled. Sailmaking was once an imperfect art, based on rule-of-thumb, guesswork and luck. Today it is a science. Sails are designed by computers, and their efficiency is predetermined.

The majority of boats today are molded of plastics, and wooden boatbuilding seems destined to become a lost art. Indeed, I wouldn't be surprised if the scientists develop a shipworm that eats only polyester and epoxy resins!

But the ancient arts of the marlinspike sailor are just as necessary in this synthetic age as they were in centuries past. Rope still requires knots, hitches and splices, and the sailmaker's sewing palm is just as useful as it was in days of old. With the new materials at our command, the application of these arts merely requires new techniques to make the fullest use of their superior qualities.

ROPE CONSTRUCTION

Except for improvements in quality and manufacturing techniques, the construction of common laid, or twisted rope is much the same as it was a thousand years ago. But despite the improvements, laid rope still has some undesirable characteristics. With extended use it tends to lose some of its twist and becomes "long-jawed." It stretches under heavy load and does not recover. It kinks or becomes fouled easily, is hard on the hands, and has a relatively short life.

Braided rope is superior to laid rope in so many respects that it is preferred by most yachtsmen, and in the author's opinion Samson Cordage Works makes the finest. Basically, it is a braid-on-braid, a diamond braid cover over a braided hollow core—a "tube within a tube." It has 25 to 40% less stretch than laid rope, has almost no tendency to kink or become fouled, reeves through blocks with less friction, is easier on the hands, and has a much longer useful life.

There is a lot of technology and control involved in its manufacture. The performance of the core must be precisely matched to that of the cover. In Samson's Yacht Braid, the cover is double-braided polyester over braided polypropylene core. The reason for mixing the two fibers is that under normal working loads the core and cover work together better than two similar fibers. Obviously, there is a different elongation between cover and core because of the helix. These differences are almost eliminated by the use of different elongating fibers, adjustment of the amount of twist, and the number of "picks" or stitches per inch.

Using Modern Synthetics in the Ancient Arts

SPLICING

It should be noted that the synthetic filaments of laid rope are quite slippery, and since good friction is a factor in the strength of a splice, certain changes in technique are called for.

When putting an eye splice in manila rope, each strand is normally tucked three times. But an eye splice in synthetic rope should have *five* tucks with each strand. Furthermore, *all* splices in synthetics should be whipped with waxed nylon where the strand ends emerge.

SEIZINGS AND WHIPPINGS

Waxed nylon small stuff is made in both laid and braided construction, replacing cotton sail twine and tarred marlin. Both cotton and hemp marlin have a relatively short life due to exposure to the elements, but synthetics are completely waterproof and weatherproof.

OTHER ITEMS

In various articles in this book, tarred hemp boltrope is specified, as in rope stropped blocks, deadeye lanyards, etc. In all instances common 3-strand laid dacron rope should be substituted, since tarred hemp boltrope is no longer obtainable in this country. In making rope mats, dacron is superior to manila, being longer lasting and cleaner looking.

Contents

Foreword V

Introduction VII

Contents IX

Making Rope Behave 1

Knot, Bend or Hitch? 3

Anyone Can Splice 7

The Short Splice 9

The Long Splice 11

The Stowage of Rope 13

How to Lay Up a Grommet 15

Whippings 17

The Heaving Line 19

Some Notes on Seizing 23

Worming, Parcelling and Serving 25

The Running Turk's Head 29

The Star Knot 31

The Tack Knot 35

The Lanyard Knot 37

Matthew Walker's Knot 39

A Simple Rope Mat 41

Ladder Mat and Block Mat 43

A Russian or Walled Mat 45

A Sword Mat 47

A Rope Ladder with a New Twist and Some Remarks
    on the Making of Baggywrinkle 49

Plaited Sennits 53

Crown Sennits 55

Rope Handles 57

Coachwhipping 59

(Continued)

CONTENTS (*Continued*)

Grafting, Pointing and Hitching 61

Cockscombing 65

The Sea Chest 67

Deadeyes and Lanyards 71

Decorative Wall Bag 73

Tom Crosby's Ditty Box 75

The Rigger's Little Helper 77

Wooden Bilge Pumps 79

Palm and Needle Practice 81

The Ditty Bag 83

The Sea Bag 85

The Bell Rope 87

Wooden Cleats 89

Rope Fenders 91

Stropped Blocks 93

Canvas Deck Bucket 95

Rigging a Jackline 97

Sail Stop Bag 99

Some Notes on the Use of "Taykles" 101

A Lanyard for a Cannon 102

The Catboat Race 105

Making a Mast Boot 107

The Water Jug 108

Registration Numbers, They Too Can Be Beautiful 109

Art and Yacht Design 110

Snythetic Fibres and Their Characteristics 115

Basic Eye Splice 117

Standard End for End 121

Back Splice 127

Index 131

Making Rope Behave

Strand

Yarns

Fibers

ROPE is probably the most remarkable product known to mankind. It is a simple thing, just a handful of fibers intertwined, its origin lost in the misty beginnings of history. Man has improved its strength, its quality, its uniformity and life, yet after thousands of years its basic construction remains unchanged.

Why then should there be any mystery about rope? Why do so many yachtsmen, when attempting their first splice, approach the task with such trepidation and fear, as though the rope were some strange complicated mechanism requiring occult powers for its mastery? Perhaps it is because they have never really looked at rope before, and have only the vaguest idea of its construction. In the ordinary handling of rope, in the splicing, knotting, hitching and using of it, it is imperative that the yachtsman have a clear understanding of just how it is put together and why. He should know all of its peculiarities, its potential powers and weaknesses. Only then can he use and care for it intelligently.

The only way to learn anatomy is to dissect a corpse, and that is what I suggest you do, the corpse being in this case a live one, a brand new piece of half inch common manila rope. It will have three strands and is commonly called hawser laid rope.

Grasp the rope with your two hands about four inches apart, palms downward. Try to twist the rope, rotating your right hand away from you and your left toward you. This tends to unlay or separate the strands. Notice that you can only move your hands a scant quarter of a turn, and when you release them the rope springs back to its original form.

The reason rope holds together in normal use and tends to retain its form under extreme stress is easy to see. The three strands are right laid, that is they spiral around the rope to the right, or clockwise. Now unlay one strand from the rope a few inches and open it up. You will see that each strand is composed of seven individual threads or yarns, which are left laid, or twisted counterclockwise. Therefore when you tried to unlay the rope you were actually attempting to lay up the yarns more tightly.

Now unlay one of the yarns. You will find it is composed of innumerable fibers of the abaca plant twisted or laid to the right. If you will examine the rope carefully you will see that every fiber runs constantly in the direction the rope lies. That is the reason for a part of its strength, and a factor controlling the amount of stretch.

So there are the three component parts of rope, fibers twisted righthanded into yarns, yarns twisted lefthanded into strands, and strands twisted or laid to the right. Each twist is made in the opposite direction to the previous twist. That is why rope holds its form, and it is the secret of its strength. The strength of a rope is far greater than the sum of the strengths of the fibers of which it is composed. It is a case of greatly increased friction acquired through twisting.

Now, having learned the lay of the various parts of the rope, it is essential that you remember to preserve the lay at all times. This means that in splicing, knotting, or any work that involves opening or disturbing the strands or yarns, you must constantly impart a slight twist in the proper direction to the part with which you are working. The beginner has difficulty in remembering this, but the expert never gives it a thought, he does it automatically. There are times when it is desirable to do the opposite, that is to unlay or untwist a part slightly in order that it may lay more fairly, but the novice should not attempt this.

There is a vast difference in the various grades of rope. Poor quality is easy to recognize. First of all it is hairy. The fiber ends stick out everywhere throughout its length, making it hard on the hands. Examine it carefully and you will see that the fibers vary greatly in size and many are looped, kinked or snarled. Likewise some yarns are twice as large as others and bunchy in spots. Finally, with such an ill assortment of parts, the finished rope lacks uniformity in its lay or twist.

Low grade rope has no place on a well found yacht. It is dangerous and undependable, aside from being hard to handle. From the standpoint of economy it is expensive, because its short life and poor service more than offset its lower initial cost.

At the other extreme is the finest manila obtainable. In the trade it is called Yacht Rope, costs more than common manila rope, and is worth the difference. To begin with, only the finest fiber and workmanship go into its making. The fibers are long and uniform in size, which in turn results in uniform yarns. The strands are smooth and symmetrical, with each yarn bearing an equal share of the load. In appearance the rope is slick and smooth, almost entirely free from protruding fiber ends. Splicing yacht rope is a pleasure because of its perfect lay and uniform quality. It reeves through blocks with a minimum of friction, is easy on the hands, and has a longer life than the common grade.

Since rope is right laid, it is always coiled righthanded or clockwise. However there is one exception to this rule. When you first handle a new length of rope it is generally kinked. To remove the kinks merely coil the rope lefthanded, then coil it righthanded. If that is not enough, just repeat the sequence. It always works.

Right here I would like to relieve myself of a minor grievance. Every book or article I have read on the care and handling of rope has advised towing a new rope overboard to remove the kinks. Now it probably will do just that. But if I ever caught a man towing a nice new manila halliard of mine overboard I'd probably either shoot him or sit down on deck and quietly burst a blood vessel. Just one of my little peculiarities.

One of the greatest destroyers of rope is rot, and rot is caused by a fungus which thrives in dampness. To prevent rope from rotting you should keep it dry and well aired. Rope that has been soaked in salt water will never dry completely because the salt in the fibers continuously absorbs moisture from the air. Granted that sheets, and halliards to a lesser degree, will probably eventually be doused by salt spray coming aboard, but why hasten the process by dumping a brand new coil of nice dry rope overboard the minute it comes aboard?

Of course anchor cables and mooring lines must be immersed and are alternately wet and dry. Rot could be a problem here, but fortunately it can be avoided by the proper treatment. There is a product known as Cuprinol, a green liquid for prevention of mildew and dry rot which is excellent. I have used it in different forms for years, not only on rope but on sails and wood, and it really does a good job. It is made in various grades for various use. For anchor cables use the grade known as Cuprinol B. C. Green, and you will not have to worry about rot.

One of the greatest enemies of rope is chafe. Cleats, chocks and blocks are responsible for most chafe. Metal cleats are one of my pet aversions because I think they are hard on rope. In the first place they are too small in their body dimensions. The rope is bent too sharply and the fibers distorted and broken. On the other hand well made wood cleats are kind to rope. There is far less friction between wood and rope than there is between metal and rope. This I can prove, I think, by an experience I had some years back.

I sailed a boat which had a bronze jibsheet cleat on the port side and a wooden one on the starboard side. Both were 6 inch cleats, the metal one of a type advertised as being an improved design. The jibsheets were three-eighth inch manila. I noticed that whenever I came in from a race there were always some minute fibers on the deck around the metal cleat, while near the wooden cleat there were none. By midsummer the port sheet was completely worn out from the constant friction of the metal, and the starboard sheet was as good as new.

Blocks also are often the cause of abnormal rope wear. Sometimes the blocks do not lie in the proper direction and the rope chafes on the edge of the shell. I have often seen mainsheet blocks which were perfectly lined up when close hauled but chafed badly when the boom was broad off. When this happens the introduction of a shackle or swivel is the cure. Jibsheet blocks are hard on rope because their sheaves are almost always too small in diameter. The constant riding back and forth over a too small sheave sets up a terrific friction between the rope fibers and shortens the life of the rope needlessly. Block manufacturers please note.

Chocks are the greatest rope eaters of all, due to the average man's customary laziness. Whenever a cable or dock line rides in a chock it should be parceled with a strip of canvas, which should be secured with marline. Let this bit of canvas take the wear instead of your expensive rope.

Good rope deserves good care. Sometime your life may depend on it. To know and use rope intelligently should not require deep study or research. All that is needed is application of a little common sense while you acquire your day by day experience. But in spite of excellent care there comes a day when rope should be replaced. The beginner generally has difficulty in recognizing the point at which it should no longer be trusted. First of all, the rope has a tired look. Throw a coil on deck and it slumps like a wet diaper.

Manila fibers contain a natural oil, and to this more oil is added when the rope is manufactured. Through exposure to the elements these oils leach away gradually and the fibers are deprived of their natural protection. Hence old fibers are soft and limp whereas they are stiff and stringy when new. Color too is an indication of rope's age. When new it is like spun gold, but as time runs on this fades to a dull yellow, and eventually it loses all color and turns a dead lifeless gray.

But by far the best indication that rope has outlived its usefulness is the condition of the fibers. Those on the surface are broken and the rope looks frayed. Open up the rope and the inside fibers will be matted and powdery.

Having determined that a rope must be replaced is no reason for throwing it away. It can still be turned into fenders and rope mats, both of which are useful aboard ship. Then if there is any left over you can give it to that next door neighbor who borrows everything and returns nothing. He may break his danged neck with it.

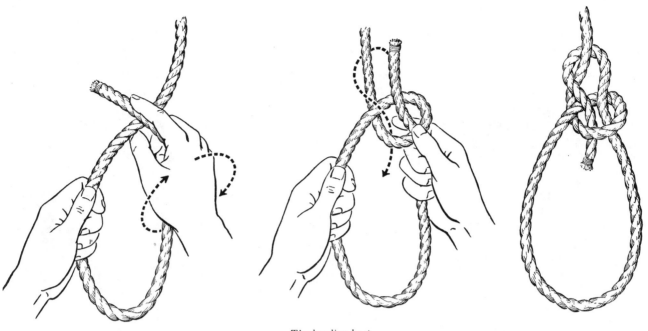

The bowline knot

Knot, Bend or Hitch?

ONE day recently I stood on the dock, watching a rather spectacular yacht race. Some seventy or more skippers were trying to get around the course under full sail in a three reef breeze. The wind was shifting back and forth as much as thirty degrees in the gusts, and wherever you looked a boat was either being dismasted or capsized or both. I noticed a cruiser towing in a small centerboarder which had been dismasted and swamped. Apparently neither skipper had a piece of spare rope aboard longer than fifteen feet, for the towline had a knot in the middle. After several nerve wracking maneuvers the operator of the cruiser managed to wallow in to the lee of a bulkhead where he crunched to a stop.

What followed was the inspiration of this article. For fifteen minutes he struggled and sweat trying to untie the soaking wet reef in the towline. One by one his fingernails parted their moorings. Finally, with a rather queer look on his face he went below, to emerge triumphantly with, as I knew in advance, a dull, rusty

knife. What happened thereafter I don't know, for I lost interest in the proceedings.

One fact, however, was brought to my mind by this performance. The average newcomer to the ever growing ranks of yachtsmen comes equipped with only a slight knowledge of rope work, and most of it wrong.

From his boyhood days in Troop C of the Boy Scouts he can only remember the clove hitch, the square or reef knot, and the sheepshank. The first will always be useful, the second has but one use, that of turning in a reef, and the sheepshank he will never need if he lives to be 100.

When he acquires a boat, be it sail or power, rope and its handling begin to play an important part in his life. He discovers it has many uses, all of which require a variety of methods for securing the rope to a variety of objects. Should he use a splice, knot, bend or hitch? There are literally thousands to choose from, and in an effort to help him learn the right from the wrong I have chosen the ones I consider most necessary to his

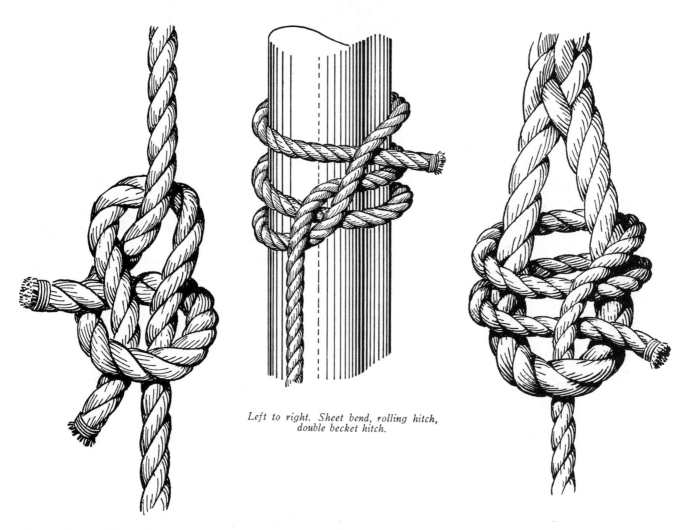

Left to right. Sheet bend, rolling hitch, double becket hitch.

day to day yachting. As he grows in years and experience he will acquire many others equally useful.

The Bowline Knot

The bowline knot is the best method of forming a temporary loop in a rope end. In fact it is the most useful knot aboard a boat. It is strong, nonslipping, and causes little distortion of the rope fibers. Even more important, it is easily untied. Rope shrinks when wet and, when under a strain in addition, a knot must be structurally perfect to untie easily.

To tie the bowline, grasp the rope end with the right hand and hold the bight in the left hand, as shown in the first diagram. Lay the rope end across the standing part and hold both parts between the right thumb and forefinger. Now rotate the right wrist away from you, bringing the end inside the loop as in the second diagram. Notice that you have put a hitch about the rope end. Without releasing the grip of the right hand, with your left hand pass the end *behind* and to the left of the standing part, and down through the hitch previously formed. It should now look like the third diagram.

There is another way to tie a bowline, but it is not as strong or secure, so I am not showing it. The method described here is the sailor's way. There are only two movements, and with practice you should be able to tie it in three seconds flat, blindfolded.

The Sheet Bend

The sheet bend is the general utility bend. For bending two ropes together it is used more than any other. It answers for almost every purpose and is easily untied. The sheet bend is similar to the bowline knot, and is tied in exactly the same manner, differing only in that one end is tied to a bight in another rope instead of being tied in its own bight. I notice that it is not too secure if the ropes to be joined differ greatly in size.

The Carrick Bend

This is an almost perfect bend. It is easy to tie, the strongest of all bends and symmetrical. No matter how great a strain has been put on it or how watersoaked it becomes, it will not jam, and still unties readily. Its only fault lies in the fact that it is somewhat bulky, but in my estimation this is more than offset by the many points in its favor.

I hardly think any instructions for tying it are needed, as the first two drawings show its construction clearly. When under strain the Carrick bend pulls up into the shape shown in the third drawing.

[4]

The most important use for the Carrick bend which comes to my mind is the joining of two towing lines or anchor cables. When a knot is going to be under a great strain, out of sight and under water too, I want to be danged sure it will hold securely and untie easily when I am through with it. Had the character I mentioned at the beginning of this article used a Carrick bend instead of a reef knot, which jams hopelessly when wet, he would not have had to dissect it with the dull knife.

The Double Becket Hitch

This is the hitch to use when bending a line to an eye splice or loop. Whalers used it to secure the whale line to the becket on the harpoon. This hitch is also excellent for bending a small rope to the bight of a much larger one. When a load is put on it, it jams up tight and never slips, yet always unties readily. It is similar in construction to the sheet bend, but has one more turn and is more secure.

To tie, bring the working end up from behind through the loop to the front, then pass it completely around the loop twice, each time going under its own part. Draw it up tightly before subjecting it to a load.

The Rolling Hitch

I prefer to call this by its original name, the Magnus hitch. However rolling hitch is easier to remember. There are many variations but this is its simplest and most used form. This is the hitch to use to attach a rope temporarily to a spar for a *lengthwise* pull. In the illustration I show it arranged for a downward pull. When attaching a tackle for unstepping a mast it would be tied upside down, since the pull would be upward.

To tie it as shown, pass the end twice around the spar counterclockwise *underneath* the standing part, then carry it above and tie a single hitch to the right. In

the illustration I have shown the three turns of the rope widely spaced for the sake of clarity, but in actual use it should be closed up snugly. Here is a hitch upon which, by the very nature of its use, your life or the safety of much valuable gear might some day depend. Therefore it is imperative that you tie it carefully, and the load should be applied gradually. Do not mistake my meaning. It is a safe dependable hitch, but since it is often applied to a smooth varnished spar it should be used with respect and not treated carelessly.

Recently I had occasion to go aloft in a bosun's chair to replace a worn pin in the masthead sheave. I was all alone. Hooking a luff tackle to my main halliard, I hoisted it aloft as far as it would go and belayed the halliard to the pin rail. With the bosun's chair hooked on to the lower block of the tackle it only took a pull of about fifty pounds to haul myself aloft. I then made fast the fall to the hook of the lower block with a bill hitch.

I middled a ten foot piece of new rope and tied a rolling hitch with it about the mast close under the masthead sheave. Since the rope was doubled, it left a bight or loop hanging down instead of the single part shown in the illustration. With my left hand over the masthead supporting my weight, I quickly shifted the hook of the upper block to the becket of the rolling hitch and gently—oh, so gently—eased myself into the bosun's chair again. This left the main halliard free of strain and I could take my time inserting a new sheave pin. Then by reversing the procedure I came down on deck safely.

The reason I mention this experience is that for twenty years I had known the rolling hitch without ever having had occasion to use it. But when the time came and only a rolling hitch would do the job, I was glad I remembered.

The Carrick bend

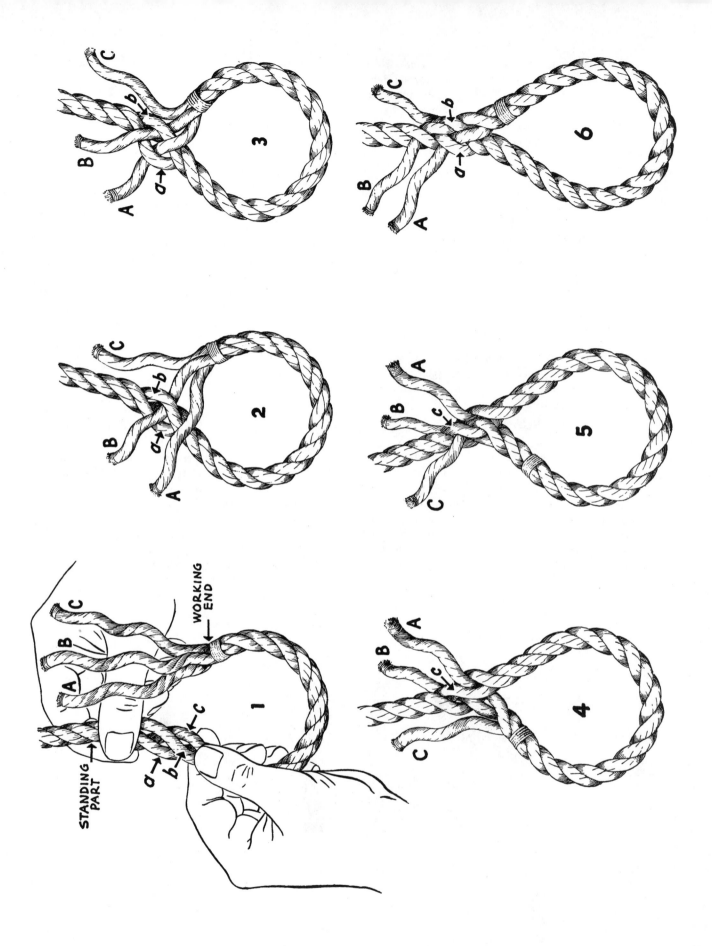

STANDING PART

WORKING END

B
C
A
a
b
c

1

C
B
A
a
b

2

C
B
A
a
b

3

A
B
c
C

4

A
B
c
C

5

C
B
a
b

6

Anyone Can Splice

SO MUCH has been written on the subject of splicing in recent years that to toss in my ha'penny's worth might seem to be useless repetition. My only defense is that newcomers who want to learn are constantly being added to the ranks of yachtsmen, and their inquiries seem to justify this effort.

For the sake of clarity the following instructions are numbered to correspond with the illustrations. So we will start with Diagram 1. Take a length of ⅜ inch manila rope and clap a seizing on about 6 inches from the end. This will be known as the working end. Unlay the three strands to the seizing and whip the end of each strand. These strands are labeled A, B and C. Note that B is the uppermost strand. Now grasp the rope as shown and twist it so the strands are opened up a bit. You now have three strands exposed which are labeled *a, b* and *c*. It is here that the first tucks are made, and since all beginners seem to go wrong right at the start you should stop at this point and study the procedure. A, B and C are the left hand, the center and the right hand strands of the working end. *a, b* and *c* are the left hand, center and right hand strands of the standing part of the rope. Strand A is tucked under strand *a,* B under *b,* and C under *c*. Just remember how the strands are paired up, left under left, center under center, and right under right.

Diagram 2 shows the first tuck. Center strand B is tucked under center strand *b,* across the standing part of the rope to the left. Remember here that you always tuck the center strand first.

Diagram 3 shows the second tuck. Left hand strand A is tucked under left hand strand *a.* Notice that it passes over center strand *b.* You are now ready to tuck strand C, but in order to do so it is necessary to turn the whole works over as shown in Diagram 4. Right hand strand *c* is now easy to get at. Strand C, although it now appears on the left side, is still the right hand strand as in Diagram 1.

Diagram 5. Strand C is now passed around to the right of and tucked under strand *c* to the left. Note that all tucks are made against the lay of the rope, or to the left. Your first row of tucks has now been made and if you have mastered the sequence the worst part is over. Before you go any further you should take out the tucks and try to do it again without looking at the diagrams. Draw all three strands up until they lie snugly, each having equal tension.

Diagram 6 shows the second row of tucks started, with strand B passed over strand *a* and tucked under the next strand to the left. Continue by tucking strands A and C over one and under one to the left. All three strands will now have been tucked twice. Tuck each strand once more in turn and the splice is completed.

Diagram 7. Your finished splice should look like this. Do not cut the strands off too close. Leave at least ⅜ of an inch protruding. Notice that all three strands have been tucked three times, and all emerge opposite one another. Lay the splice on the floor and roll it back and forth under your foot. This will even up the strands a bit and make the splice symmetrical.

These drawings and directions are as clear and simple as I know how to make them. They are directed to the beginner, and for that reason I have not mentioned the finer points such as tapering, etc. In splicing, as in everything else, practice makes perfect and in the doing you will learn more than from reading any ten books on rope work.

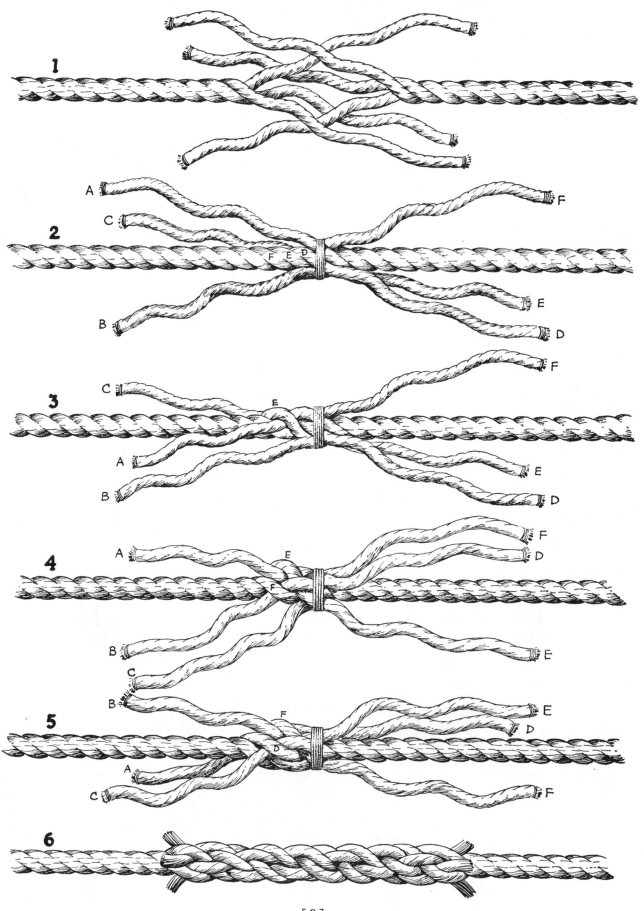

The Short Splice

SOME years ago a rigger in the Brooklyn Navy Yard made up an eye splice in ½ inch wire rope for me to use in teaching marlinespike seamanship to a group of beginners. It was one of the most beautiful splices I have ever seen. In fact it was perfect. But for my purpose it was useless. Each strand and every wire was so carefully tucked and positioned that even an expert would have difficulty in tracing out the sequence of the tucks and the method of tapering.

Therein lies the reason why it is difficult for an artist, striving for perfection, to produce a drawing of a splice which will be clearly understandable to the beginner and yet pass the critical eye of an expert. Consider the illustration of the short splice at the bottom of the opposite page. In order to clearly define the lay of all the strands it was necessary to distort and exaggerate them, resulting in a lumpy, uneven and unprofessional looking splice. In other words, it is a fairly good (to the beginner) drawing of a perfectly lousy (to the expert) short splice. All this is by way of explanation to those same experts, who might reasonably assume that I don't know what a good splice looks like.

But let's get on with our knitting. Every yachtsman should know how to make three splices—the eye splice (which has been covered in a previous article), the short splice, and the long or running splice. The short splice doubles the diameter of the rope at the point of joining and is used mainly in lengthening dock lines, towing hawsers and ground tackle. For sheets and halliards, which must pass through blocks or fairleads, the long splice is used since it does not increase the diameter of the rope.

To practise splicing, ⅜ inch rope is the size to use. It is small enough to tuck easily, and large enough to prevent distortion. For the short splice take two pieces about 2 feet long and carefully unlay one end of each piece 5 inches. Put a temporary whipping on the end of each strand and clutch them together as shown in illustration No. 1. Note that each strand of one rope lies between two adjoining strands of the other rope.

Now bring them together snugly, as shown in illustration No. 2, and clap on a narrow seizing where they join. This seizing should be as tight as you can make it, so don't use grocery string. Incidentally, there are some who will tell you that the use of temporary whippings and seizings when splicing is unnecessary, and the mark of an amateur. Don't believe a word of it. It is more often the sign of a careful worker who takes pride in his work.

Illustration No. 3 shows the first tuck. Strand A is passed over strand D, which lies next to it, and is tucked under strand E. In other words, the sequence of tucks is over one and under one, as in the eye splice.

Illustration No. 4 shows the second tuck. Strand B is passed over strand E and under strand F. The splice should be rotated *away* from you one-third of a turn before making this tuck.

Illustration No. 5 shows the third tuck. Rotate the splice away from you another third of a turn. Pass strand C over strand F and tuck under the next strand, which is D.

You have now completed the first round of tucks in the left hand half of the splice. Continue by tucking each strand once more, over one and under one. Go back over your work and see that each strand lies snug and fair, with no kinks, and all three strands have been drawn up with equal tension. Now make another set of tucks as before, and one-half of your splice is finished.

Turn the whole works end for end so that strands D, E and F appear at the left instead of the right. This brings them into the position of strands A, B and C in the illustrations. Now proceed to make three rounds of tucks with strands D, E and F exactly as before. When finished, remove the seizing from the center, place the splice on the floor and roll it back and forth under your foot. Cut off the ends of the strands, leaving at least ¾ of an inch protruding.

If all has gone well, your splice should look something like illustration No. 6. It will not look very fancy but it will be safe, in fact almost as strong as the rope itself. Two things would help improve its appearance. One is to slightly *untwist* the strands when tucking them, and the other is to taper the strands. This last is an art in itself and one that I hope to cover in a later article.

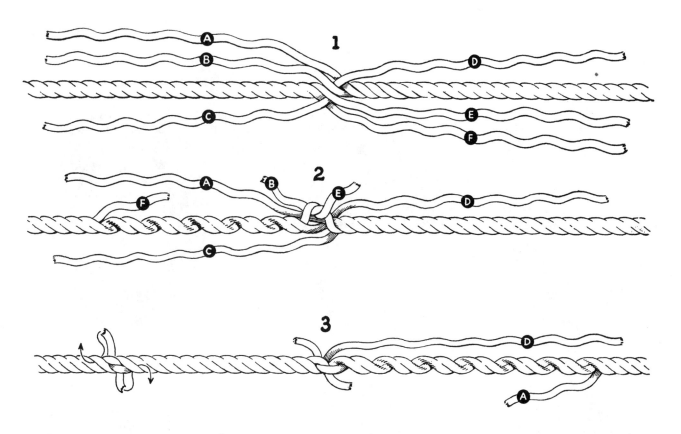

The Long Splice

NO YACHTSMAN can lay claim to a complete education unless he can make a long splice. While it is true that he will seldom have need for it, there are times when nothing but a long splice will meet an emergency. It will pass through a block or fairlead where a short splice would jam. If a halliard or sheet parts because of chafe or injury, the long splice is the answer. Why throw away a hundred feet of good manila rope because six inches of it is worn out?

A long splice is considerably weaker than a short splice and therefore should be approached with a careful hand and a prayerful attitude. Let's assume you have half inch rope. To begin, unlay very carefully the strands of both ropes a distance of 15 to 18 inches, more if your rope is larger than half inch. Try to preserve the lay of the strands and disturb them as little as possible. Then clutch them together *closely,* as shown in the first illustration, just as you do for a short splice.

Referring to illustration No. 2, tie an overhand knot *loosely* with strands B and E. Note carefully the *direction* in which the strands are passed in making the knot. Now unlay strand F 10 or 12 inches further to the left. (This is considerably further than the illustration shows, since space limitations prevented drawing it to scale.) Next, lay up strand C in the groove formerly occupied by F. When

strand C meets strand F, join them in an overhand knot just as you did with B and E, but this time draw the knot up tight. Untwisting the strands slightly in the way of the knot helps to keep it from becoming too bunchy.

Now go back to the knot in strands B and E and draw it up snugly. Examine your work carefully at this point, for right about here is where beginners generally go haywire. Unless all three strands in your finished splice are laid up evenly, with equal tension, the job is a failure, and it will probably give way or part when subjected to a load. It is hard to describe or picture. You have to see or feel it. If your knot is drawn up too tightly, the other two strands do not carry their share of the load and the splice fails at that point. If the knot is too loose, the strength of the splice is reduced by one-third.

Referring to illustration No. 3, unlay strand A 10 or 12 inches and lay up strand D in its place, then tie an overhand knot as before. If, after examining your work, you are satisfied that all three strands are laid up evenly, proceed to dispose of the ends of the strands at each knot. There are several ways to do this, but the commonest is to tuck the strand over and under, as shown by the arrows at the left. After tucking, cut each strand off, leaving at least one-quarter of an inch protruding. Roll the splice under your foot before cutting off to smooth it out.

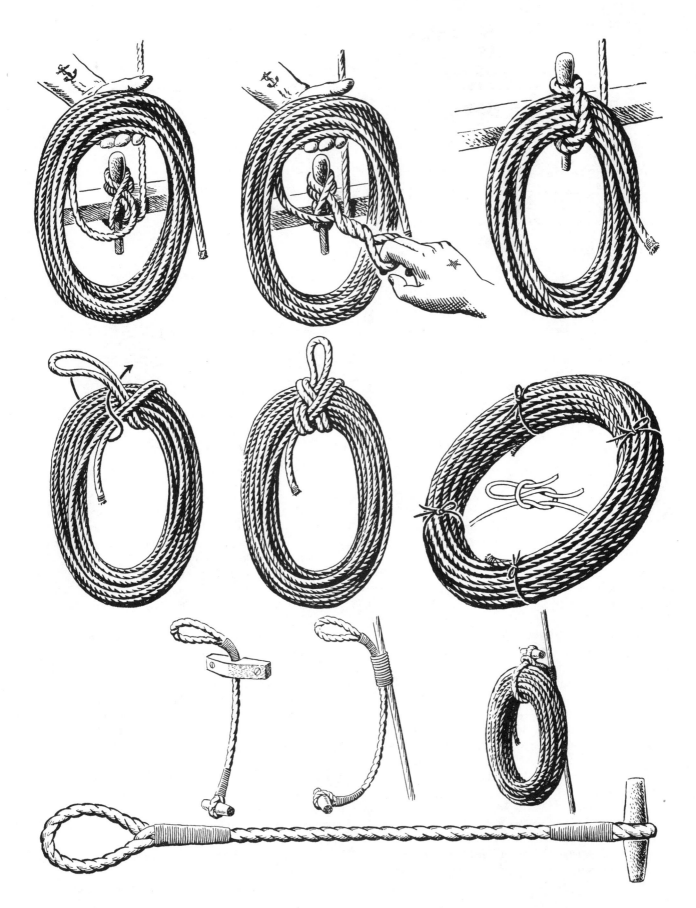

The Stowage of Rope

THERE IS an ancient saying I am prone to quote when called upon to justify my somewhat fanatical interest in marlinspike seamanship. "By his ropes ye shall know the measure of the Sailor." A little meditation on the thought expressed therein leads to the conclusion that it is just as applicable to the astute yachtsman of this modern day as it was to the illiterate seaman who wandered about the seven seas 300 years ago. A sloppy ill kept ship is ever the mark of a poor sailor and an indication of indifference or ignorance or both. But a competent man learns early in his career that his life and the safety of his ship depend on orderliness. "Shipshape, Bristol fashion" may sound quaint to the uninitiated, but it packs a world of meaning.

Above all else a good sailor hates loose gear, be it rope, boat hook or bobby pins. He knows that at all times every item of gear not in actual use should be stowed away or secured. He has learned that sheets and halliards must be ready to run clear in an instant, without fouling. He knows he may have to pay out 100 feet of cable in a hurry on a dark night, and is prepared to do so. He realizes that if and when he needs life jackets there will be no time for pawing around up in the forepeak or dismantling a made-up berth to get at them. He has a place for everything and he *keeps* them there, with a catalogue in his head. In the most accessible places are the items he will need quickly, and he is darned sure they are ready for instant use.

These are but a few thoughts that occurred to me when preparing the drawings for this article. To one whose entire experience has been in sailing craft loose gear generally means rope in some form or another. Bobby pins are just a danged annoyance, but sheets, halliards and cables are a matter of vital concern at all times.

We can assume that every yachtsman knows how to coil rope. He knows that right laid rope is always coiled right handed or clockwise, and the only time he coils it left handed is in the case of new rope, when he wants to get the kinks out. What we are concerned with here is what he does with it *after* it is coiled.

Once a sail is hoisted, and the halliard is belayed to its cleat or belaying pin, the excess rope is carefully coiled, always starting at the cleat or pin and working outward to the bitter end. Now just dropping the coil on deck in the immediate vicinity is very bad practice and poor seamanship. Sooner or later wind or water will skid it down into the lee scuppers, hoplessly fouled. Another practice which is far too common is to jam the coil in between the standing part of the halliard and the mast. This is the mark of a landlubber, and the lad who does it should be put on bread and water!

The first three illustrations show how to dispose of a coiled halliard sailor-fashion. After the coil is made up it is held in the left hand close by the cleat or pin. Then reach through the coil with your right hand and pull the bight next to the cleat or pin through the coil. Now twist the bight 3 or 4 times to the left, lay the coil against the turns on the pin and slip the twisted bight over the handle of the pin, or the upper horn of the cleat as shown in the third illustration. The twisted bight should be no longer than is necessary to encircle the coil and slip over the pin, thus locking the coil in position. When ready to lower away, the bight is slipped off the pin, the coil is dropped on deck face down and the chances of fouling are rare indeed.

The next two illustrations show how to make up a coil for hanging. It is basically a storage coil for hanging up spare gear below decks or ashore. Although there are many different methods of doing the same thing, I have used the one shown here for many years and it has proven entirely satisfactory. It is neat, secure, easy to tie and untie, and has a loop for hanging. A bight is formed near the bitter end and a hitch is taken to the right snugly around the top of the coil, and then a second hitch is taken to the left. Notice carefully that it greatly resembles a clove hitch, which it is not! This coil will stand considerable handling without loosening up.

When it comes to stowing an anchor cable we have a different problem, because it is so bulky that hanging is impractical and it is necessary to stow it flat. The next illustration shows the obvious solution—at least four, and often five, stops of marline tied with a *slipped reef knot*. Thus the coil is confined about its circumference and the stops may be yanked off in an instant.

The last illustrations show a piece of gear seldom seen nowadays. It is a toggle and becket straight from a square rigger. If seized to a shroud or cleated to a bulkhead or coaming this takes care of your dock lines or other coils of spare rope. It is a short length of quarter-inch cotton rope spliced around a grooved wooden toggle with an eye splice in the other end. The coil is placed in position and the toggle is brought up in front and buttoned into the eye. There are no knots to tie, the coil is held securely, and it can be cast off in an instant. A pretty neat affair, I call it.

So if you would be known as a good sailor, make up your coils with extreme care. Remember you always have time to coil a rope, but you never have time to clear it when it is fouled, because it is then much, oh much, too late.

How to Lay Up a Grommet

IN LOOKING over the articles I have written I noticed that many of the items of ship's gear which I have described call for the use of grommets, called "grummits" by all true sailors. Many yachtsmen having an elementary knowledge of marlinspike seamanship are familiar with grommets and their uses, but I have observed that most of them get about as far as Figure 3 of the accompanying illustrations and then hopelessly bog down, with only a vague idea of the proper way to finish the job. This article will, I hope, relieve them of their distress.

Grommets of stranded rope, marline and wire have many uses aboard ship. They are the straps, or "strops", of the old fashioned blocks, the beckets on sea chests, hatch lifts, drawer pulls, and the eyelets in canvas work of the old school. To the landlubber they are quoits. Technically they are rope rings formed by laying up a single strand about itself 3, 4 or 6 times. As in the case of block straps, they are often wormed, parceled and served over.

A 3 strand rope grommet requires a single strand whose length is 3 times the circumference of the desired grommet, plus 6 times the circumference of the rope. Thus a ⅜ inch grommet 6 inches in diameter calls for a single strand approximately 64 inches long. This allows about 3½ inches to each end for tucking.

From a piece of rope the required length unlay carefully a single strand without disturbing the lay of the yarns. Bring one end around to form a ring the desired diameter, and cross the strand as shown in Figure 1.

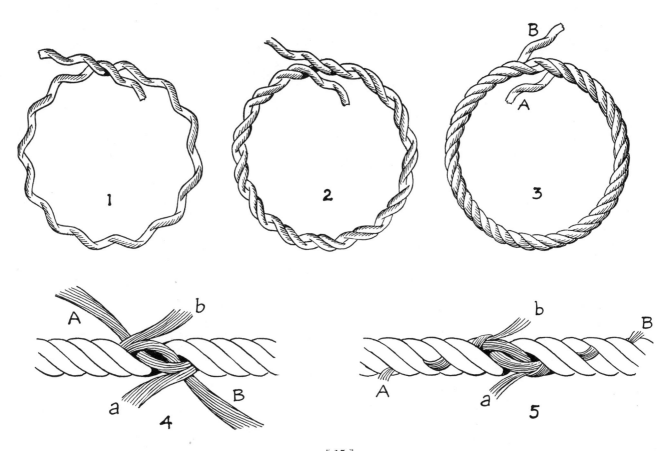

Now pass the long or working end about itself one complete circuit of the grommet as in Figure 2. This, of course, is fairly obvious, but if you get a bit careless the two adjacent strands may not match, and a botched job will result. In the groove remaining lay up the strand for another circuit as in Figure 3.

You are now faced with the problem of disposing of the two strand ends, the object being to tuck them in such a manner as to increase the diameter of the rope as little as possible. This is done precisely the same as in a long splice. To my knowledge there are fourteen ways to do it. Six are used by sailmakers, and the rest by riggers. To show them all would be a superfluity, to use an awk-ward word, and I have chosen a method that is simple, neat and entirely practical.

Unlay each strand slightly and separate into two parts or groups of yarns. Now with one-half of each strand tie a *left-hand* half knot, as shown in Figure 4. Strands A and B are now to be tucked, and strands a and b are temporarily ignored. You tuck over one and under two. Strand A goes over B and b, and under the next two strands, then tucked once more. Strand B goes over A and a and under two in a like manner. It should now look like Figure 5. Roll the grommet in the way of the tucks under your foot, or wallop it a few times with a mallet and cut the strands off close.

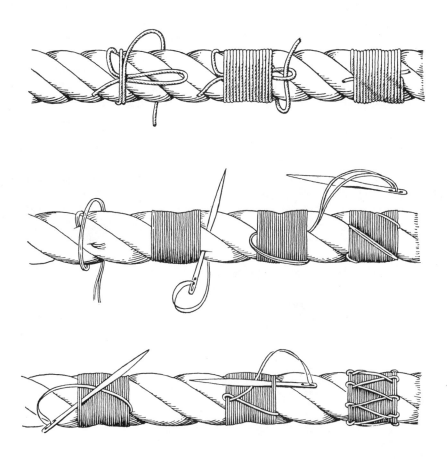

Whippings

THE practice of whipping rope ends is so elementary that it hardly seemed important enough to justify a chapter on the subject. But then I thought of all the cowtails I have seen, the haphazard windings of grocery string, the tricky back splices which refused to pass through blocks, and it was obvious that missionaries are still needed to carry light to the heathen.

The purpose of a whipping is to prevent the rope from unlaying, and insure that the rope end will at all times pass quickly and easily through blocks, fairleads or eyes. There is also the matter of pride. "By his ropes ye shall know the measure of the seaman." Frayed rope ends are a curse and an abomination, but no more so than improperly made whippings, for they indicate either ignorance or indifference. Ignorance is excusable and

often temporary, but indifference generally becomes a bad habit.

Your ditty bag should hold several kinds of whipping material for different kinds and sizes of rope: a spool of first quality sail twine, generally obtainable only from your sailmaker, some strong fish line in the smaller sizes, and a ball of Italian tarred hemp marline. If you are a perfectionist you'll use nylon thread for whipping nylon rope, and linen thread for linen rope.

Whippings, like seizings, are always made *against* the lay of the rope. Remember the old saying, "Worm and parcel *with* the lay, serve the rope the *other* way." How many turns make a whipping? Enough to equal the diameter of the rope. Half inch rope gets a whipping one-half inch long, one-quarter of an inch from the end. Actually the correct way is to place the whipping several inches back from the end and cut off the rope after you have finished. For a first class job always shellac the whipping and you will find it will generally stay intact for the life of the rope.

Illustration No. 1 shows a plain or common whipping on 4 strand rope. It was made with a hard-laid fish line. This is the simplest and quickest of all whippings and will do in a pinch when you have not much time, but it has a habit of coming loose when subjected to much handling. If you like a good job well done, do not consider this one for anything but a temporary whipping. I think the illustration explains itself. The standing end is laid along the rope in a loop, a number of turns are taken about it, and the free end is passed through the protruding loop. The left hand end is then pulled until the free end is drawn in to the center of the whipping, and both ends are then trimmed off.

Illustration No. 2 shows the palm and needle whipping, the best by far of all. No matter how much use or abuse the rope is subjected to, it will not work loose or come off, even if many of the strands of the whipping are cut or chafed through. Thread a needle with a doubled length of twine and take a stitch through a strand of the rope to anchor the end. After a sufficient number of turns have been made pass the needle through a strand, emerging in the contline between the strands as shown. Now pass the twine up across the whipping diagonally and stitch back through the next strand, emerging in the contline, thus in effect forming a worming over the whipping. Draw the twine up snugly and continue around the rope. If you want to make it even better, go around a second time, thus forming a double worming. To secure the end, shove the needle clean through the rope before cutting off.

Illustration No. 3 shows a snaked whipping. You may call it a fancy whipping, and so it is when applied to man ropes or yoke ropes. But actually its prime purpose is to protect the ends of large stuff—cables or ropes over one inch in diameter. Put the whipping on with needle and twine as before, stitching through a strand when finished, and then take a hitch about the *two* outside strands, alternately across to the left and right as shown.

The Heaving Line

"CAPT'N AL," asked the small boy, "what's a heaving line?"

"Why that's a lifeline for sailors when they's seasick," the captain replied.

"But what's the ball on the end for?"

Capt'n Al shifted his pipe to the port side of his other tooth. "It's a gag, son, just a gag!"

Believe it or not, there are a surprising number of yachtsmen who do not own a heaving line, have never used one, or do not even know what it is. It is true that one may sail for a dozen seasons without meeting a situation requiring its use, but when that day comes the heaving line may save a life and every well found yacht carries one on deck where it is handy. Every yachtsman should know how to make one and how to use it. An hour's practice on the lawn is sufficient to acquire the proper technique in throwing it.

Bradford's *Glossary Of Sea Terms* defines a heaving line as "a light line weighted at its end to aid in throwing to a pier or another vessel, as a messenger for a heavy line." In my opinion most yachtsmen can lay their craft in to a pier close enough to toss a dockline ashore, and those who cannot probably are inexperienced and could not throw a heaving line anyhow. But even the expert has been known to stall a motor or get in stays, and when that happens a heaving line can prevent serious damage to both his pride and his yacht.

More important, to my mind, is the use of the heaving line in going to the aid of craft in distress. It generally happens in foul weather, a capsized sailboat with three kids hanging on her rail, or a motor boat with dead engines and wallowing broadside in the trough. You want to put a line aboard without damaging either your or the other fellow's boat, and with rough seas and a high wind such a task calls for seamanship. While approaching, the heaving line is bent to a cable or towline and then coiled carefully, the coil held loosely in the left hand, and the weighted end swinging in the right. You come up to windward of the disabled craft, thus making a lee for him, and the wind helps to carry the line straight to him. An underhanded swing does it, and do not swing it around your head like a cowboy if you want an accurate throw.

A proper heaving line should be about seventy-five feet long for a yacht of moderate size, longer for a large vessel. It should be light enough to throw easily, yet strong enough to haul a man through the water, and five-sixteenths inch manila is about right. In order to give weight to the end of the line so that it will carry some distance a knot of considerable size is required. Since time immemorial the monkey's fist has been the standard knot used for this purpose, and no one has been able to come up with a better one.

To make the monkey's fist lay a bight of the line across the fingers of the left hand, about three and one-half feet from the end, holding the standing part with the left thumb. Take three turns about the fingers, which are separated as shown in the first illustration on the following page. Now take three turns at right angles, as in illustrations 2 and 3, through the fingers and about the first three turns. At this point the knot is removed from the fingers and a third set of three turns is made about the second set, and inside the first set. The fourth illustration shows this final step, and alongside is the finished knot with all the slack taken out.

Now this results in a knot that is roughly cube shaped and rather small, hollow inside. It lacks the weight necessary for throwing any distance, so it is necessary to load it. This is accomplished by placing a rubber ball, a smooth round stone, or similar spherical weight inside the knot before it is worked taut. A ball of lead foil is ideal, for it can be made as heavy or light as you choose. This is a problem calling for serious thought and delicate judgment, as the heavier the weight, in reason, the easier it is to throw, but out of consideration to the man on the receiving end who will catch it in good faith there is the question of how much weight shall be called sporting. So be sure it is heavy enough, but do not lay yourself open to charges of premeditated mayhem.

When the knot is loaded and drawn up firmly it assumes a spherical shape, and you should have an end about eighteen inches long protruding. This end is brought down alongside of, and side spliced into, the standing part. Then a seizing is clapped on both parts close up under the knot, and don't forget to put a

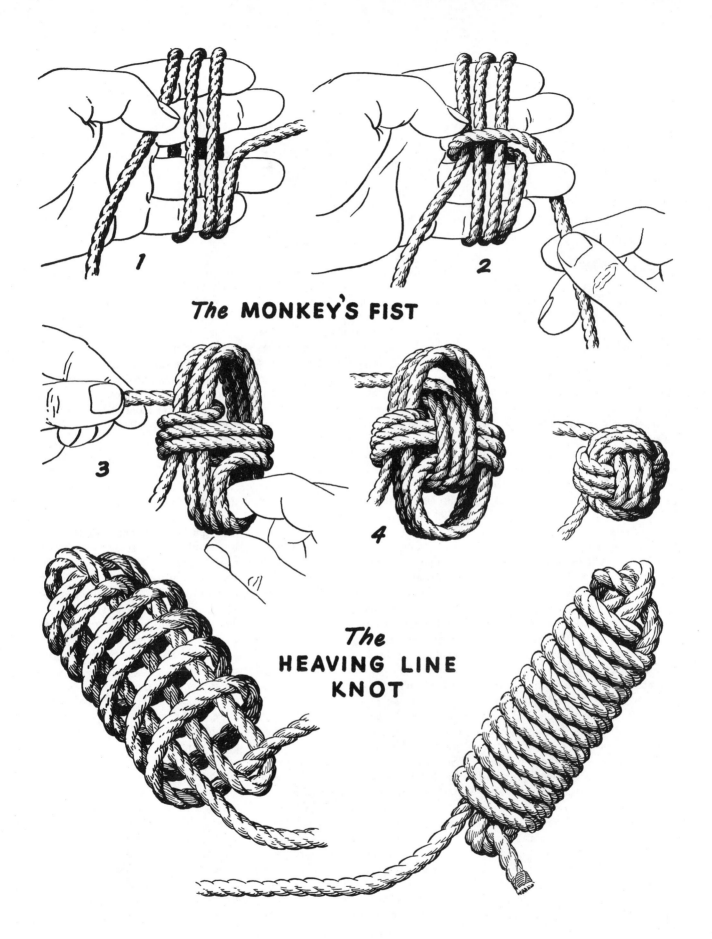

The **MONKEY'S FIST**

1

2

3

4

The **HEAVING LINE KNOT**

palm-and-needle whipping on the other end of the line.

Next I have shown a heaving line knot, which is derived from the hangman's knot. This is often found in use on ferryboats, barges, etc., and is a little too sloppy for use on yachts, but I have a purpose in mind which I think justifies my showing it. Let us assume you need to throw a line some distance in an emergency and no heaving line is handy. Grab the nearest coil of three-eighths or one-half inch rope and tie this knot in the end. It can be tied in less than fifteen seconds (try it) and gives the bulk and weight necessary for a good throw. However use it only as an emergency measure, for

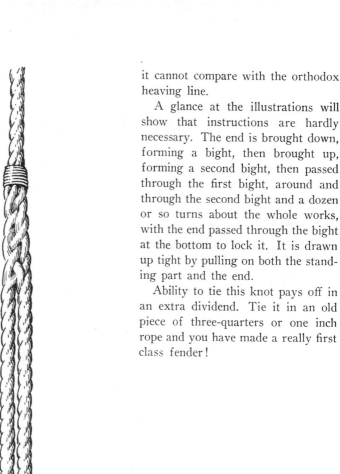

it cannot compare with the orthodox heaving line.

A glance at the illustrations will show that instructions are hardly necessary. The end is brought down, forming a bight, then brought up, forming a second bight, then passed through the first bight, around and through the second bight and a dozen or so turns about the whole works, with the end passed through the bight at the bottom to lock it. It is drawn up tight by pulling on both the standing part and the end.

Ability to tie this knot pays off in an extra dividend. Tie it in an old piece of three-quarters or one inch rope and you have made a really first class fender!

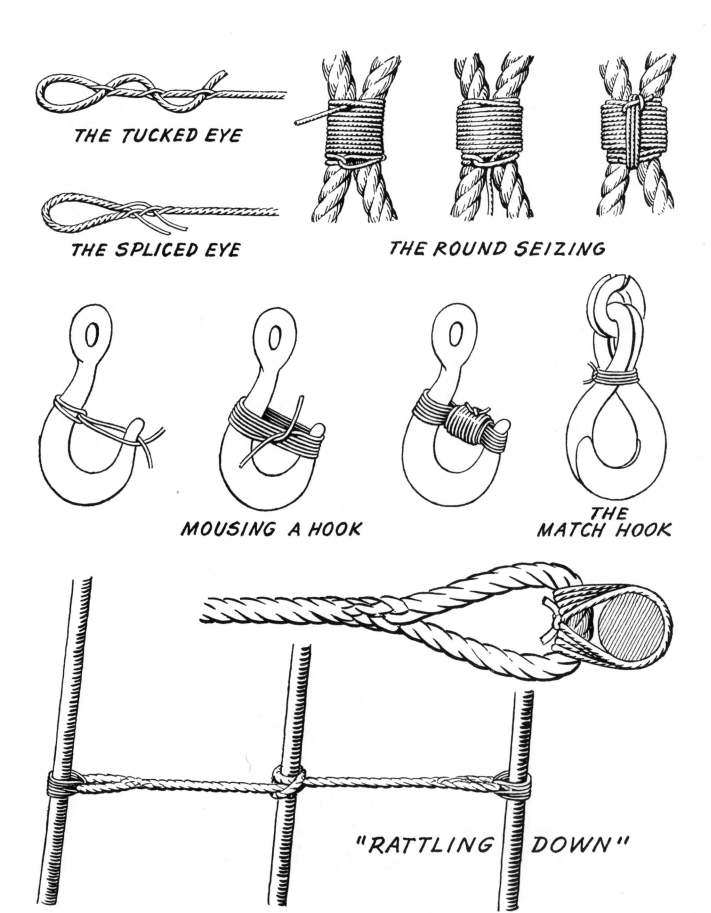

THE TUCKED EYE

THE SPLICED EYE

THE ROUND SEIZING

MOUSING A HOOK

THE MATCH HOOK

"RATTLING DOWN"

Some Notes on Seizing

THE rigger's art is a combination of many skills, the practice of which is dominated by two factors, tradition and experience. Each job must be done a certain way. Ask the rigger why, and he'll probably say "B'guy, I dunno. I allus done it thataway 'n I don't know a better way. But lemme tell you one thing, no job a-mine ever let go!" What he means, although he doesn't know it, is that his method was acquired through tradition, and its superiority was proven by experience. It is with this in mind that I hereby assert my deep reverence for tradition, and I shall always be a missionary spreading the gospel according to Matthew Walker.

A seizing is a simple thing, and because it is so elementary it is rarely given the attention it deserves. In splicing, rigging and the making of ship's gear it is used by every yachtsman, generally incorrectly, and often in a slipshod manner. Why not take time out and look into the subject a bit?

Seizings are made with small stuff, generally tarred hemp of two strands, laid left handed. Marline is the most commonly used, and the smallest. The largest seizing stuff is hambroline, which is three strand right laid. Marline is something one should buy with care, the best of which is known as yacht marline, the finest grade of imported Italian tarred hemp. It is small in diameter, exceedingly strong and weather resistant. Domestic marline is lumpy, poor in quality, and short lived, only good for seizings of a temporary nature.

The first thing to plant firmly in your mind is the method of starting a seizing. Seizings of marline or small stuff are generally started with an eye. Now there are two ways to form an eye in marline, both of which are shown on the opposite page. Most men have large fingers, and find difficulty in handling very small things. For them the tucked eye is the easier method. Just twist the marline to unlay it and tuck the end through between the strands several times as shown. Leave the end rather long, and if the tucks and the end are buried under the first few turns of the seizing it will be most secure. An eye can be formed in this manner very quickly.

The spliced eye is a bit more involved but neater and more secure. The drawing shows the procedure, and only a couple of tucks are necessary.

Having settled the matter of starting, let's look at the round seizing, the most used and most practical of all seizings. You will probably use it to form an eye in rope. First draw the two parts together with the looped marline. Then put on ten or twelve turns, working upward towards the eye of the rope, and finish off with a single hitch as shown. Now working downward apply a second layer of turns over the first, but two less in number. These are called riding turns and should always be used for a permanent seizing, but if it is of a temporary nature they may be omitted. A seizing without riding turns is called a flat seizing.

Now pass the end of the marline through the tucked or spliced eye, between the two parts of the rope to the back, and around the riding turns three or four times as shown in the third illustration. These turns are known as crossing turns, and are hauled as taut as possible, then secured with a single hitch.

You will often have a deck block secured to an eye bolt with a hook. This calls for a seizing of some sort to prevent its coming adrift. Here the seizing is called a mousing. To mouse a hook double a length of marline and secure with a bale sling hitch to the back of the hook as shown. Separate the two strands and bring them around the bill of the hook on opposite sides. Now pass them around eight or ten times, cross them in the middle and, working outward with each strand, apply frapping turns as tightly as possible. Then work back to the middle again with riding turns and finish off with a reef knot. This method of mousing a hook has been in use for 300 years and is still the best.

I have shown a match hook, sometimes miscalled a sister hook. This too calls for a seizing to prevent the two halves from separating or shaking loose. In this instance there is no great strain on the seizing itself, so all that is needed is a flat seizing, the ends secured with a reef knot.

Ratlines are generally associated with square rigged vessels, but more than a few yachts carry them. If your yacht is rigged in a manner permitting their use they are a great convenience and highly desirable, particularly in cruising. Here too tradition governs the method by which they are installed.

Custom decrees that shrouds are always said to be "rattled down", but for what reason I do not know, since you always "rattle up". Ratlines are made of light tarred hemp rope, three strand. In service they are periodically retarred for weather protection. They have an eye splice in each end which is seized to the forward and after shrouds, and are clove hitched to the intermediate ones. The drawings show the method of seizing and the finished job. Note that the eye splices are seized in a horizontal plane.

Before rattling down, the shrouds must be parceled and served their entire length with marline, thus providing the necessary friction to prevent the seizings from slipping. The ratlines are spaced anywhere from thirteen to seventeen inches apart, fifteen being customary, and are leveled off by lining up with the horizon. The ratline is first clove hitched to the intermediate shrouds on the outboard sides, and then the eyes are spliced in so they barely meet the forward and after shrouds. The ends are seized with tarred small stuff generally heavier than common marline, and the large illustration shows how the turns are laid on.

Yes, I admit that "clapping on" a seizing, as it is properly called, is a very minor detail of marlinspike seamanship, but nevertheless it is important that it be done right. I am only human, and like everyone else I am inclined to slight the small jobs when pressed for time. Often I have turned out a sloppy seizing or whipping because of a more urgent or important matter. But somehow the danged thing keeps staring me in the face and following me around, and then I get to thinking of my great grandfather revolving in his grave like a pinwheel. So I sit right down and do the job over, first class, shipshape and sailor fashion.

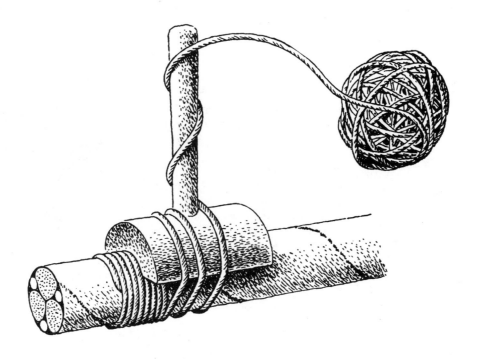

Worming, Parceling and Serving

OF THE many and varied skills practised by the ship rigger of olden times quite a few have survived by virtue of their practical application by the yachtsman. One of the most important of these is the subject of this article—the service of rope. Hempen standing rigging gave way to wire rope several generations ago, and deadeyes and lanyards are but rarely seen today, but as long as man puts to sea under sail there will always be a need for splicing, serving and whippings.

Worming, parceling and serving are the means by which rope is protected from wear through chafing, or from rotting due to the entrance of water.

Worming is the laying-in of marline or spun yarn between the strands of rope, spirally and with the lay. It is done to fill the grooves or hollows between the strands, thus giving the rope a smoother firmer appearance.

Parceling is the wrapping of narrow strips of tarred canvas around the rope after worming, spirally and with the lay. Each turn of the canvas overlaps the previous turn, and so prevents water from entering the rope strands.

Serving is a continuous tight winding of marline about the rope against the lay, after worming and parceling. When rope has been given these three treatments, it is stronger, much stiffer, protected from chafe, and if tarred or painted is completely waterproof. Needless to say, it is only applied to standing rigging.

Before proceeding one should memorize the old time sailors' ditty:

> "Worm and parcel with the lay,
>   Turn and serve the other way."

It is only rarely that present day yachtsmen have occasion to worm a rope. Its use is generally restricted to the eye in a heavy dock or mooring line. However it should be noted that in decorative rope work worming is often applied externally over a stitched-on canvas covering. Common applications are man ropes, yoke lines and chest beckets, which when given several coats of white paint are quite handsome.

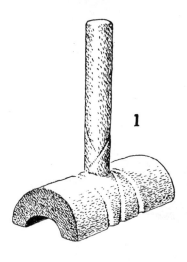

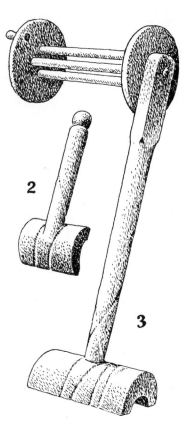

Parceling should always be applied before serving. While canvas is the accepted material, common electrician's friction tape is preferred for small size manila and for wire rope. It is waterproof and adhesive, and makes a good tight foundation for the serving. Bowsprit foot ropes of small size wire should be heavily parceled with canvas before serving. The idea here is not the protection of the wire, but rather to build up the diameter to insure good footing. Only the most rugged can stand for long on ¼ inch wire in bare feet! Where parceling is employed without serving, such as chafing gear on a mooring line where it rides in chocks, the canvas is always wound against the lay of the rope, and is secured with marline hitched-on or seized.

Serving is the most useful skill of all, particularly for the neck of eye splices. Eye splices in manila are served with tarred marline, often without parceling, to prevent the tucks from loosening and to give a handsome appearance to the splice. In wire rope the splice is parceled and served to cover protruding wires and to bind the individual strands together tightly, thus increasing the friction and strengthening the splice. Splices in galvanized wire rope are generally served with marline, but in stainless steel the serving is of annealed stainless wire.

It is impossible to put on a good serving with the hands alone, and mechanical means are needed to get sufficient tension. For this we use a tool known as the serving mallet. As shown in the illustration, several turns are taken about the rope by hand, then the marline is passed around the head of the mallet several times and then twice around the handle. Grasping the handle, the mallet is rotated about the rope against the lay. The friction of the marline on the handle controls the tightness of the serving. This gives tremendous leverage, and only experience can teach you how to achieve the proper tension. Actually your ears can help, for the friction of the marline on the mallet sets up a continuous squeaking sound if handled correctly.

I have shown my four favorite mallets. Numbers 2 and 4 are properly called serving boards, for their handles are offset from the heads. Number 1 is a common type for general use. Number 2 is a very small one for serving small eyes, being but two inches long. Number 3 is a mallet with a wooden reel to

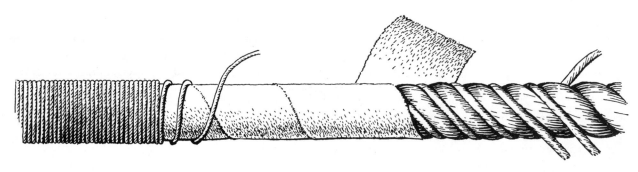

hold the marline. This enables one to do a job single handed, for it is obvious that without a reel a helper is needed to pass the ball of marline around the rope as the mallet is rotated. With this type the number of turns of marline about the handle determines the tension, for the mallet is not grasped in the hand but literally spun around the rope. It is really a great deal of fun to use.

Number 4 was made by Capt. Tom Crosby in 1854 of whale ivory. It is five inches long and obviously made for very large rope, for the hollow of the head is very shallow.

Serving mallets are generally homemade. They should be made of a very hard close grained wood such as lignum vitae or locust, for the friction of the marline is so great that it quickly wears deep grooves in anything softer. Mallets for serving with wire are made of metal, preferably brass.

My suggestion is that you sail offshore immediately, harpoon a sperm whale and knock out one of his bicuspids. It would make a well nigh perfect serving mallet!

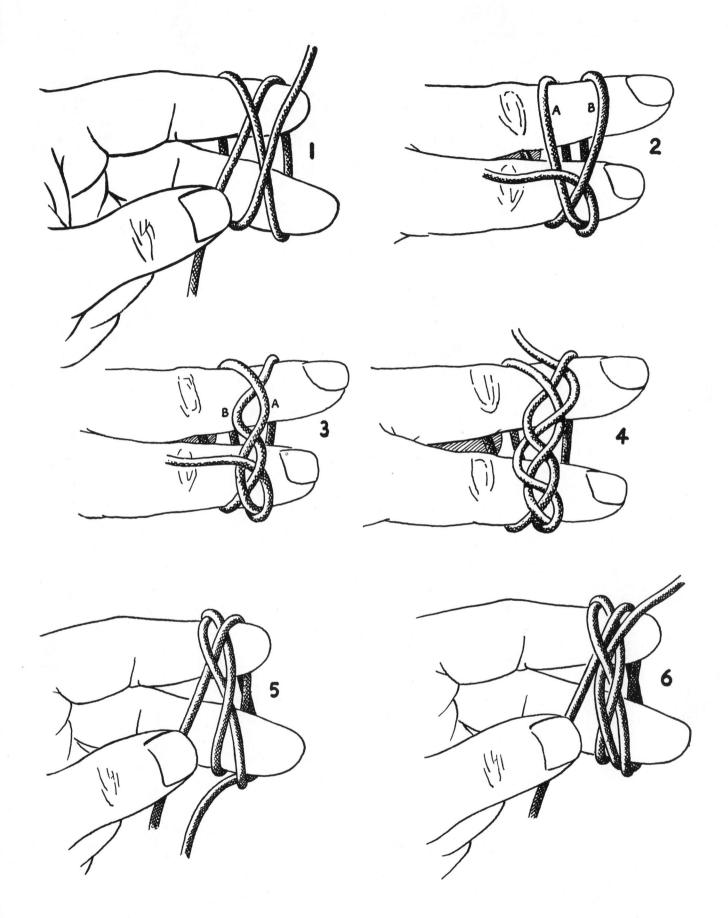

The
Running Turk's Head

ONE of the most ancient of all decorative knots identified with the sailor, and also the most common, is the Turk's head. Being relatively easy to tie and remember, adaptable to many uses and possessing a beauty of form and character distinctly its own, its popularity is readily justified.

There are well over a hundred different kinds of Turk's heads, most of which are so elaborate and involved that their tying becomes an intricate stunt rather than a useful accomplishment. Few yachtsmen have the time or the interest required to master them, but every one should know the knot in its elementary form. Applied to stanchions, yoke ropes or tiller, it adds an authentic touch of detail to one's yacht and gives her character. Sea chest beckets, bell pulls, ditty bag lanyards, the steering wheel, all need the Turk's head. Spaced six inches apart on bowsprit foot ropes, they give better footing when handling headsails. One lad to whom I introduced the knot presented me with a Turk's head ring, made of fine silver wire painstakingly laid up into three strands. Yes indeed, the Turk's head knot belongs to the sailor!

I have found that one-eighth inch braided cotton line makes a good looking Turk's head and is easier to handle than stranded stuff. In most stores it is sold as flag halliard. If the knot is for outside use exposed to the weather it should be shellacked and painted white when finished.

To start, hold the standing end with your thumb and pass the working end twice around your fingers as shown in illustration No. 1. Rotate your fingers toward you, and tuck the working end as shown in No. 2. Pull bight A across to the right and bight B under A to the left. It should now look like No. 3.

The working end is now tucked through bight B toward you, then over A to the right and up under the bight directly above. It should now look like No. 4.

Rotate your fingers away from you to their original position and you'll find you are right back where you started, but the knot is now "set up" and should look like No. 5.

Now tuck the working end alongside the standing end, as in No. 6, keeping always to the right of it, and following it over and under around your fingers until you are back again where you started. You will now have a Turk's head of two passes, and since you need three, proceed to pass the working end over and under once more, again to the right of the previous passes. This sounds confusing as I write it, but it is easy when you have the line on your fingers and the tucks then become pretty obvious.

Having finished your tucks, the next step is to take out all the slack in the strands, starting at one end and working round and round the knot, until every part has equal tension and symmetry. The ends are cut off underneath the strands so they do not show.

The Star Knot

PERHAPS the most distinctive of all sailor's decorative knots, the star knot, has been known and admired for over 150 years. Since it is somewhat on the intricate side it has never been commonplace, for out of every ten sailors who could work a manrope knot, as an example, probably but one knew how to make a star knot. Thus today, as in yesteryears, having the star knot in one's repertoire is a mark of distinction, placing the sailor a step higher in the social scale than his fellows. Indeed, the thought fascinates me. I can picture hundreds of yachtsmen looking disdainfully down their noses at their shipmates and sneering, "Just a wall and crown sailor. Phooie!"

The star knot has many uses. As the terminal knot of a bell lanyard it has no equal, and when tied in the end of a short length of ¾ inch rope it makes a lethal weapon to be respected. It is most commonly found in sea chest beckets, and is worked with 3, 4, 5 or 6 strands. I have chosen the 5 strand for demonstration because it is undoubtedly the handsomest of them all. Once having learned it, the others are a cinch since their basic construction is the same.

There are many variations of the star knot, most of which involve the superimposing of wall or crown knots, but I believe there is a limit to the amount of interest the average yachtsman has in decorative rope work, and the basic star knot is elaborate enough for all practical purposes. I suggest you make one of 3, 4, and 6 strands, for besides seeing for yourself how the character of the knot may be varied, the repetition of the procedure will implant itself in your mind so firmly that you will always remember it.

In the planning of these illustrations I have kept foremost in my mind the trouble I had in mastering this knot. All the books I had consulted suffered the same deficiencies—inadequate descriptions and atrocious illustrations. Eventually, and with considerable profanity, I learned how it was done, and was surprised (also burned up) to discover it was nowhere near as difficult as the books would have you believe. Being an artist by profession, I believe in graphic instruction, that one good illustration is worth more than ten pages of description. Therefore in the present instance I have constructed a star knot, broken it down into its component parts, and have drawn exactly

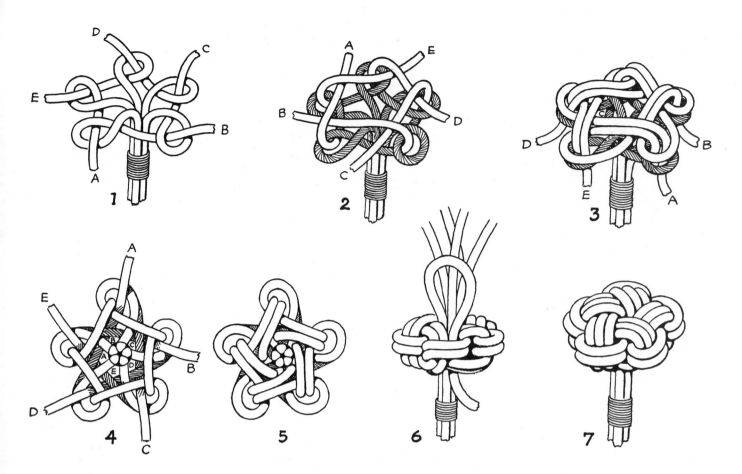

what I saw in my hand, step by step. The strands have been designated by letters, yet I honestly do not think it necessary other than that it helps to tie them in with the description.

The difficult thing about all knots is not in the making, but in *remembering* how it was done. Since practice makes perfect, the answer is obvious, and I think you will find that after you have made three 5 strand star knots you will not soon forget the sequence.

The best material for knot practice, as I have often stated, is ⅛ inch braided cotton line, flag halliard stuff. Cut 5 pieces about one foot long and seize them together near one end. This end shall henceforth be known as the stem. Now with the palm of the left hand held upward, push the stem down between the first and second fingers and arrange the 5 strands radially. With the right hand strand of the 2 nearest you, take a hitch around the left hand strand. Working to the right, take the next strand and make a hitch around the second strand. Continue by hitching the fourth strand around the third and the fifth around the fourth. Finally pass the end of the fifth strand through the bight of the first. In other words, "make like the first illustration".

Now crown the 5 strands *to the left,* as shown in illustration 2.

For step 3, still referring to illustration 2, strand A is passed to the left around the bight of E, then under its own part to the right parallel to strand B on the inner side, over strand C, and the end is then tucked down through the bight at the lower right "corner". Strand B is next passed around the bight of A, then under its own part along the inner side of C, over D, and the end is tucked down through the bight at the upper right. Continue in like manner with the rest of the strands, when your work should then look like illustration 3. If it does, remove the knot from the left hand and turn it upside down so that you are looking directly at the stem of the knot, when it will look precisely like illustration 4. If it does not, you had better go back and start all over.

Now bring strand A (illustration 4) forward, parallel to the adjacent strand, and tuck it down through the center of the knot alongside of the stem. Do likewise with the other strands, working to the right or counterclockwise, and it must look like illustration 5. Study the present step very carefully, because it is easy to go haywire at this point. However, the knot commences to take form at this stage, and the strands will tend to assume a logical position.

Next turn the knot right side up again, with the strand ends protruding from the top of the knot at the center. Illustration 6 shows this, with one strand started in the final tuck. Each strand in turn is tucked as shown, emerging at the bottom of the knot alongside the stem, where it is then trimmed off close. Take particular notice that the strand passes under 4 parts—the 2 strands which form the rim, thence back towards the stem under the 2 bottom strands. Illustration 7 shows the completed knot with the strands cut off.

There is one point I would like to stress which will help in the tying of this or any other knot of 4 or more strands. In the setting up of the knot, or in its early stages of formation, draw the strands up rather snugly at each step, even though there does not seem to be room enough to make the next tuck. This helps you visualize the form of the knot, enables you to keep track of the strands, and to spot mistakes easily. The star knot in its initial stages, if done loosely, resembles a rat's nest or a spaghetti dinner, and when you get so confused you are apt to become disgusted and give up the whole project. I still insist that all knots are easy to make, provided you have a clear picture of each step, and are not in a hurry.

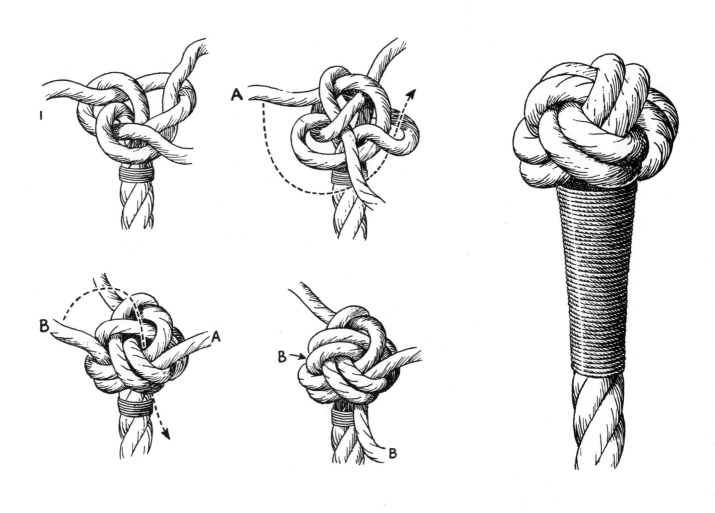

The Tack Knot

EVERY yachtsman having more than a passing interest in marlinespike seamanship should know at least one decorative end rope knot. Its usefulness will depend on the amount of ship's gear he makes himself. It should be simple to make, easy to remember and handsome in appearance. These specifications narrow the choice down to a handful from possibly several hundred.

End rope knots are, as the name implies, formed with the end of stranded rope for the purpose of raising a knob. They are found in bucket ropes, bell pulls, sea chest beckets and, for those who wish to commit mayhem, cat-o'-nine-tails.

I have chosen the tack knot because, with minor variations, it can be adapted to many different uses. The knot as shown here, with the three strands tapered and served,

is admirably suited to the end of a bucket rope, and will often prevent the loss of a good deck bucket when used under way. Tie the same knot in four strand rope, but cut off the strands close under the knot and you have a manrope, or topsail sheet knot. Basically it is a wall and crown, doubled. When used for purely decorative reasons the strands are separately covered with canvas before tying, and the knot is painted when finished.

To practise tying this knot take a piece of ⅜ inch rope and put a seizing on about 8 inches from the end. Unlay the strands and whip the ends. Now lay up the strands as shown in drawing No. 1, which is a single wall knot. Do not draw up the knot tightly, but just enough to hold its form.

Now tie a single crown knot on top of the wall knot,

as shown in drawing No. 2. Note that the strands constantly travel in the same direction, that is counterclockwise. If you were to draw the knot up tightly you would see that in itself the single wall and crown is a neat compact knot. However it lacks bulk, and so we double it. Each strand in turn is led around its own part of the initial wall knot. Still looking at drawing No. 2, lead strand A around outside of and below itself, and out through the next bight, as shown by the dotted line. Do likewise with the remaining strands. You now have a double wall and single crown, and it should look like drawing No. 3 (I hope).

To double the crown each strand continues alongside of its own adjacent part, but instead of tucking through the next bight, it is passed straight down through the body of the knot, emerging at the bottom alongside of the standing part of the rope. The dotted line, No. 3, shows how, and No. 4 shows one strand passed.

Now proceed to take the slack out of the knot by pulling up each strand in turn, all around the various parts, until it is firm and symmetrical. The strands are left about 2 inches long and scraped to a taper, then wormed into the standing part and tightly served over.

To tie the knot in four strand rope the procedure is the same, but the result is much more beautiful.

The Lanyard Knot

THE lanyard knot is tied in the standing end of the lanyard, and is placed at the left hand hole of the upper deadeye, inboard of course. It is a perfect stopper knot and is of fairly recent origin, having superseded the Matthew Walker knot, formerly used for the purpose in the early 1800's. Lanyards are always four strand tarred hemp, well greased before setting up.

There are several methods of tying a lanyard knot, most of them based on the Matthew Walker, but the one I am showing is in my opinion the easiest to remember. Fundamentally it is a wall knot, or perhaps I should say two wall knots, interlocking.

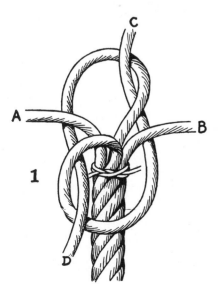

To start the knot put a temporary seizing on the rope at least one foot from the end, and unlay the strands carefully to the seizing. Bend the left hand strand out to the left and the right hand strand to the right. In the first illustration I have designated these two strands A and B respectively. For the time being we will disregard them. Now with the other two strands, C and D, tie a wall knot underneath the first pair, enclosing the body of the rope. Leave the wall rather loose, as I have shown it in the first illustration.

Now bring down the first pair of strands, A and B, and wall them underneath the first wall, as shown in the second illustration. Note that A and B come up through the bights formed by C and D. Thus all four strands emerge from the center of the knot. Carefully draw up the strands and take up the slack, working the knot down onto the seizing as you do so. Finally heave hard on each strand so that the knot is tight and symmetrical.

Next lay up the strands into four strand rope again, carefully imparting a good left twist to each strand as you lay it up. Now work a tight palm and needle whipping close to the knot, and cut off the rope end cleanly.

You will probably get a perfect knot on your first try, so the next

problem is to remember it. Just reduce the procedure to its simplest terms, about as follows: "Wall two opposite strands under the remaining two, then wall them under the first two, with every strand tucked through two bights."

Even if you do not go to sea with deadeyes and lanyards, the lanyard knot is worth knowing. It is excellent for rope handles, beckets, and rope handrails, or wherever a stopper knot is called for.

The Constrictor Knot. Right about here is a good place to recommend the world's best temporary seizing, the constrictor knot. It was invented some thirty years ago by the late Clifford Ashley, whose lifetime of research in knots has never been equaled. Wherever a seizing or whipping of a temporary nature is desired,

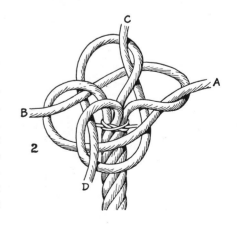

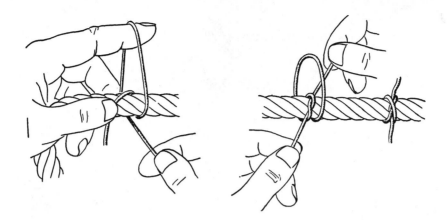

this is the answer to a sailor's prayer. The harder you pull it the tighter it grips. In fact, once set up really tight, it is almost impossible to untie. It is quicker to cut it.

The constrictor knot is simplicity itself—just a righthand halfknot with a riding turn added. As shown in the illustration you start with a round turn about the rope, held with the thumb and second finger, then a second round turn is taken about the rope and the raised index finger of the left hand. Now bring the working end up over and under the standing end in a right halfknot, as in the second illustration. Pull it up carefully and tightly as the twine will stand. Note how the riding turn bisects the halfknot and keeps it from slipping. With two riding turns the knot makes a pretty good whipping, although it will not last as long as the orthodox whipping.

This knot should not be confused with a similar knot called the strangle knot, which is almost the same thing. In the strangle knot a left-hand halfknot is used, and it is nowhere near as secure.

Having plugged the constrictor knot, I will henceforth specify it in lieu of the indefinite term of "seizing". Once you get used to this knot it is amazing how many uses you will find for it, one of which immediately comes to mind. It would make an excellent necktie, properly drawn up, for that moron in a speedboat who loves to tear through a crowded anchorage at dinnertime.

Matthew Walker's Knot

IN THE year 1808 there was published in London the first comprehensive and complete book on the subject of marlinspike seamanship, *The Sheet Anchor* by D'arcy Lever, the foremost authority of his time. Illustrated by quaint but remarkably clear and concise woodcuts, it was for a hundred years the sailor's Bible, and for a hundred years its contents were borrowed, lifted, copied and pirated by all and sundry without hindrance. Today it is a collector's item, rarely obtainable, and at a price that would astound its long deceased author were he alive to collect.

It is in this book that we find the first printed reference to the Matthew Walker knot, presented by Lever as a "handsome knot for the end of a lanyard." It was superseded by the lanyard knot *per se* which I described elsewhere. Of Matthew Walker, the man, absolutely nothing is known, and many are the legends perpetuated explaining his origin, all of them just so much bilge water. Experts refer to him as "the only man ever to have a knot named for him." Even this intriguing statement will not hold water, for both Napoleon and his girl friend Josephine had their names given to knots. You will recognize the Josephine knot by its more commonly used name, the Carrick bend, and the Napoleon knot is merely a larger, more elaborate development of the same.

Therefore about all we can say of Matthew Walker with any degree of authority is that he probably was a sailor and that he invented the excellent knot which bears his name. Whoever he was, I wish I had known him. Requiescat in pace!

Of the knot itself we could write a book. Specifically it is a stopper knot used to form a knob in a rope's end. As a lanyard knot, which I have shown in the first illustration, it is tied always in four strand rope, and the strands are laid up and whipped as shown. But unless you are one of those rare individuals who go to sea with deadeyes and lanyards, your use of it will be as a stopper knot to be applied to sea chest beckets, bucket ropes, bell pulls, etc. For these and other uses it can be tied with any number of strands from three to twenty-four or more, although eight are about all a normal man would care to handle unless he were getting paid for it. There are so many ways to tie it and to finish it off handsomely that I have had a difficult time choosing the simplest and most practical way to present it, but since it has always been my earnest intention to reach the reader who is new to the game I have necessarily choked off a yearning to "tell all." When you are nuts about knots it is hard to avoid excess verbiage.

For practice take a length of three strand three-eighths inch rope and apply a constrictor knot as a seizing about ten inches from the end. Through an oversight I failed to show this in the illustrations, for which I apologize. Unlay the strands to the seizing, and tie a wall knot with the left hand strand A, as shown in the first diagram. Note that the strand encircles the rope and comes up through its own bight, thus forming a left hand halfknot. Now take the center strand B and wall it as before, as in the second diagram. Observe carefully its position. It comes down in front of strand A, encircles the body of the rope below A, and finally comes up through the bight of A as well as through its own bight.

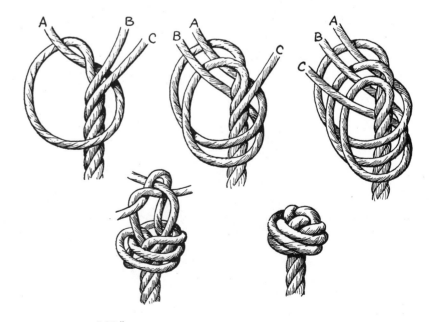

Next wall strand C in the same manner, but this time the end comes up through all three bights, A, B and C. The third diagram shows the sequence clearly. The first strand A passes through one bight, the second strand B through two bights, and the third through three bights. This, then, is the basic structure of all Matthew Walker knots, regardless of the number of strands used. All you have to remember is that each successive strand must pass through the bight of each previous strand in sequence. For instance were you tying a four strand knot, the fourth strand would pass in turn through the bights of strands A, B and C, and finally through its own bight.

At this point I suggest you practice drawing the knot up into shape before we get into the technique of disposing of the strands. First arrange the strands so that they emerge fairly from the exact conter of the knot. Then proceed to draw up the slack of each strand in turn, a little at a time, until the knot is firm and solid. The hard part is in working the knot down solidly against the seizing you originally applied to the rope. Now to finish the knot off as a lanyard knot, as in the illustration at the end of this chapter, lay the strand ends up tightly again into rope and apply a palm and needle whipping close to the knot and cut the ends off smoothly.

As a stopper knot or a decorative rope end knot the strands are generally crowned and then tucked down through the center, which gives a rather handsome finish. Here the procedure is a little complicated. Look at the fourth diagram. After the initial knot has been set up draw the strands up *partially,* just enough for the knot to begin to assume its final form. Now crown the protruding strands loosely as shown, tuck each one down through the center of the knot and arrange them uniformly around the body of the knot. Then go back and draw the Matthew Walker up tightly into its finished shape. Lastly take each strand end beneath the knot and draw up the crown until it is seated snugly on the top of the knot as in the final illustration. Caution—in drawing up the crown do not pull too hard or you will sink it right down through the body of the knot. The strand ends are cut off close where they emerge beneath the knot.

You should achieve a pretty fair knot on your first try, but I suggest you make half a dozen or so, using different sizes of rope. By the time you are finished with them the procedure will be firmly fixed in your mind and you will have done your part toward perpetuating the memory of a man named Matthew Walker.

A Simple Rope Mat

WHEN reeving off a new set of sheets and halliards your typical yachtsman will invariably make up the old ones into neat coils and hang them up in the garage or boathouse, there to gather dust and spiders. He will do this year after year, and eventually will have accumulated quite a collection of old rope too poor to use and too good to throw away.

One of the best ways to make use of that old rope, and to keep yourself occupied during the long winter evenings, is to work up a complete set of rope mats for the boat. On the bridge deck and at the foot of the companionway the decorative oval ones are most suitable. In the cockpit, where firm footing for the helmsman is more important than eye appeal, a wrought or sword mat is the type to use. Then there are fancy ones of white cotton for the ladder steps, thump mats of the Turk's head type for sheet or traveler blocks, and many others.

Capt. James H. Berry, who was quartermaster on the Henrietta in the great ocean race of 1866 at the age of seventeen, and who later sailed with Hank Haff in the America's Cup races, rigged out his house fore and aft with rope door mats like the one shown here. As a boy I always wiped my feet on them carefully and reverently,

for here lived a real sailor who had been places and seen things! And to top it off, he was my grandfather. Come to think of it, I guess he is sort of responsible for this article.

So let's start with the fancy oval mat first, which is nothing more than a triple-passed Napoleon knot in the middle of a Flemish coil or fake, and is made of ⅜ or ½ inch rope.

Take a bight about 12 feet from one end of a 35 foot length and proceed to set up the knot as shown in the three diagrams. The arrows indicate each succeeding step. Lay it up loosely so you can clearly follow the over and under sequence. When finished according to the third diagram, you will have a single passed knot with one short and one long end, both coming out the bottom.

Now take the long end and pass it alongside the short end, all through the knot, until you come out again at the starting point. You now have the same knot, somewhat tighter, only the parts are doubled. Continue all around through the knot once more until you again reach the starting point, and you will have the triple-passed knot as shown in the mat. However it will appear loose and flimsy, so take a bight anywhere and start to take up the

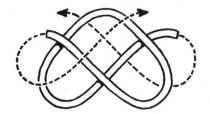  

The three steps in setting up the Napoleon knot

slack, working in both directions all through the mat. This is the part that consumes time, so take it easy. The beauty of this and similar knots lies entirely in their symmetrical shape, the smooth even lay of all their parts, and the absence of bulges or distortion. This is only achieved by working with care and patience.

Cut off the surplus rope so the ends lie side by side separated by a single strand or part. These ends should be sewed fast to the body of the knot.

Now lay the knot on the floor with the rope ends uppermost. Whip the end of another length of rope and start laying it up in a snug coil about the knot. Of course the more rope you coil the larger the mat, but 3 feet the long way is about the limit for this type of mat, so add another length if needed with a long splice. When you reach the desired size cut the rope off opposite the point where you started the coil, and on the same side of the knot. Unlay the strands for about a foot and taper them by scraping with a knife, being careful not to disturb the coil.

Lay them up again into a rat-tail, whip the end and sew fast to the coil with sail twine. Then go back and sew the end you started with to the edge of the knot against which it lays.

Obviously something is needed to hold the mat together. So thread a large sail needle with marline and sew through each rope in the coil from the knot to the outer edge radially, then along the edge about 3 inches and back through the coil again to the knot. Reverse and continue until the whole mat is sewn together, the strands of marline running outward like the spokes in a wheel.

The mat is now complete. Turn her over and see how she looks. The rope ends in the knot cannot be seen, nor should the marline stitching. Does the knot look lumpy? Take a wooden mallet and sock it a few times. Anyhow it will smooth out with use.

If you have taken sufficient care to lay up the knot and coil snugly, with an even tension throughout, the mat will be symmetrical, firm and smooth. It will be nonskid, wrinkleproof, long wearing and good looking. And you'll have used up some of that old rope you were saving.

The marline stitching passes through one strand only in each rope

Fig. 1

Ladder Mat and Block Mat

MARLINESPIKE seamanship, fascinating though it may be, is too often misunderstood and misused. To many it denotes fancy ropework indiscriminately applied to everything in sight with no apparent purpose but to display one's cleverness. Traditional customs of the sea are deserving of preservation and worthy of one's sustained interest. But adaption calls for a certain amount of discretion. After all, it is a long way from a five boat whaler of 1840 to a thirty foot modern auxiliary.

Used with restraint, fancywork has a definite place even today, but let's be sensible about it. Do not consider an item unless you are sure it will serve a useful practical purpose. Turk's heads were not worked on foot ropes to make them pretty. Their fancy appearance was only incidental and secondary to their prime purpose, which was to keep one's feet from slipping.

The ladder mat shown in Figure 1 is another case in point. Companion ladder steps are invariably covered with corrugated rubber matting. Now I will admit it is no doubt entirely practical and efficient, but to anyone with an eye for beauty rubber matting is uninspiring and totally lacking in design or character. Neat rope mats, however, are not only just as efficient but softer

under foot, far more interesting, and bespeak a real welcome to the cabin below.

The design shown here is the sailor's true lover mat weave. Only white cotton rope should be used here. Lay it up loosely as the diagram, Figure 1A, indicates, following the over-and-under sequence carefully. Then pass one end all around two more times, always keeping on the same side of the other strand. Now gradually draw up the slack a little at a time until the mat is symmetrical, uniform and compact. Arrange your two ends to come out on the under side and sew them fast.

The mats should be secured to the ladder steps by nailing all around the edge with brass escutcheon pins.

Fig. 1A

Fig. 2

Fig. 2A

Use a nail set to sink the heads down into the strands.

If your boat has sails it also has deck blocks. They rattle and bang on the deck and eventually will wear holes in the canvas or mar the brightwork, to say noth-

ing of the wear and tear on your ears. The best answer to this problem is a thump mat placed around the eye bolt underneath the block, as shown in illustration Figure 2. It is a perfect shock absorber, noise reducer, and incidentally an eye catcher.

For this job I would use nylon rope. A mat such as this will be watersoaked more often than not, and if made of cotton or manila might tend to curl up cup-shaped and would discolor quickly. Nylon would lay flat and stay brighter longer.

Lay it up with the aid of diagram Figure 2A, then pass it through two more times and work out the slack. Secure the ends by sewing them fast on the underside. Unshackle your block and slip the mat over the eye bolt, and the result will dress up your ship no end.

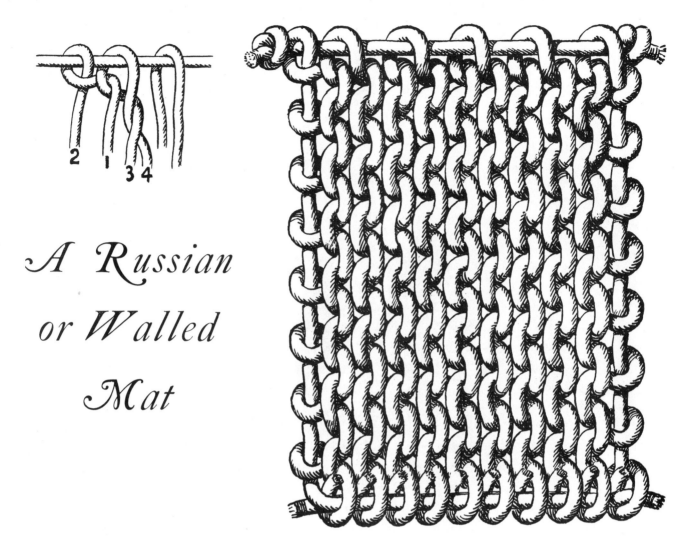

A Russian or Walled Mat

FOR a good looking nonskid cockpit floor covering there is nothing better than a Russian or walled mat. It is long wearing, holds its shape well, and can be made any size you desire. It is not too difficult to lay up. All you need is time, patience and a lot of rope.

Quarter inch is the best size rope for this type of weave. Anything heavier would make the mat appear coarse and clumsy. I find that quarter inch braided cotton sash cord is ideal. It makes a smooth neat mat, and is easier to lay up than a laid rope.

You start by stretching a head rope breast high between two convenient points. Haul it taut and secure. Over this head rope, middle a suitable number of strands. Now starting at the left side, bring strand 1 forward, to the left of and over in front of strand 2 (of which it forms a part), then forward through the bight of strand 3. Take strand 3 through the bight of 4, and continue by walling each strand in turn to the right through the bight of the following strand until you reach the last strand. To turn the corner, pass the *next to the last* strand in back of, around, and in front of the last strand. Then start walling again, this time to the left. Continue until the mat is the desired length, merely by walling across first to the

right and then to the left. Note in the illustration that the outside strand on the left, and the outside strand on the right, are used only as filler strands.

To finish off, pass these filler strands across the bottom and hitch the other strands around them. Pull each strand through tightly as you hitch, and cut it off. The head rope is now cut down and the ends either half knotted, or walled and crowned and then trimmed off close.

Your first attempt with this mat may result in a sad looking mess. As you wall across the mat the weave may get tighter or looser; and as if this were not enough, the free ends begin to get fouled up and you start to sweat and cuss. However don't let it get you down. Just unlay the whole dang thing, stoke up your pipe, and start all over again. It takes practice, but once you get the proper "sequence of fingers" you will notice that there is a rhythm to it, and the mat builds up rapidly.

One last point. Don't expect anyone to tell you how much rope it takes to make a mat. That would make it too easy. You will have to guess at it like the rest of us, and learn the hard way. Besides it's more fun!

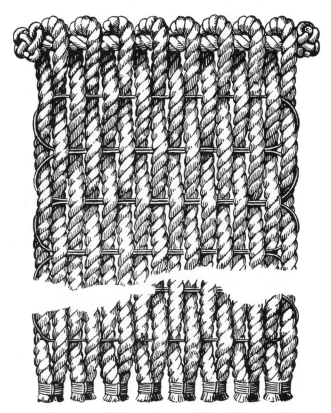

A Sword Mat

OF ALL the various types of woven matting made and used by seamen sword matting is undoubtedly the oldest, for its construction is that of the most ancient of fabrics—a simple warp and filler. Generally made on a crude loom, it was used aboard ship in the old days for chafing gear and gaskets.

For the present day yachtsman it has several applications. A strip along the side deck amidships gives ample protection from hefty females in high heeled shoes and boatyard mechanics in steel shod brogans. A narrow strip along the rail cap where you haul the dinghy aboard will save wear and tear on both the dinghy and the rail.

Making a loom for a sword mat is a little involved and hardly worth the effort for the man who only wants a few pieces. It can be woven quite easily by hand right on the floor, provided you stick to narrow widths.

So let's assume you want a strip about 15 by 30 inches. Take 20 pieces of ⅜ inch rope about 6 feet long and middle them over a short head rope or lashing. Lay the whole thing out carefully and evenly on the floor. Stretch the headrope taut and tack each end of it to the floor as shown in the diagrams. Now starting with the first rope or strand on the left hand side, lay each alternate strand up over the head rope. Let's call these the A strands.

Middle a 60 foot length of heavy marline or tarred cod line and make up each end into a ball or skein. Now lay the bight of it across the strands close up in the crotch formed by the A strands and the other group labeled B. Put your foot on the marline at one side of the mat and pull it taut with the opposite hand. This leaves the other hand free to manipulate the strands.

Next lay the A strands down over the marline and carry the B strands up over the head rope.

Pass the marline across from each side and again draw it taut, holding it with your hand and foot as before. Continue by bringing the B strands down and laying up the A strands, and again crossing the marline.

Try and keep the marline at an even tension throughout, close up in the crotch of the two sets of strands, so that the finished mat will be close woven and firm. For the sake of clarity the illustration shows the weave much looser than it should be. When you "reach the end of your rope", reef-knot the ends of the marline together and seize the rope ends together in pairs. Finish off the head rope with a single wall and crown at each end.

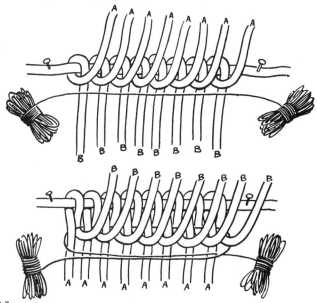

A Rope Ladder
with a New Twist

And Some Remarks on the Making of Baggywrinkle

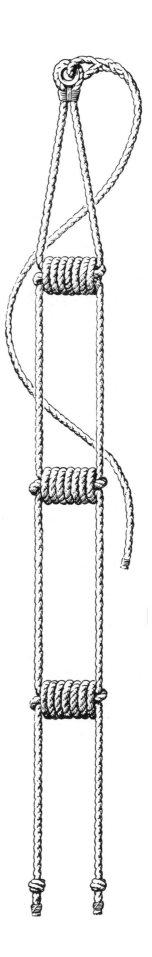

ALMOST every yachtsman at some time in his career feels that he must have a rope ladder, primarily for swimming from his boat. This is a perfectly logical desire which can be satisfied in two ways. He can walk into the nearest marine supply store and buy a serviceable rope ladder for less than ten dollars, or if he's so constituted he can take some salvaged material and spend seventy-five dollars worth of time making his own. It is to the man who chooses the latter method that these remarks are directed.

Common rope ladders have wooden rungs or steps and are called Jacob's ladders, have been used for centuries as boarding ladders, and in modern times as swimming ladders. Generally speaking they are bulky and awkward to stow, although otherwise very practical. However the ladder I am showing here is definitely not a Jacob's ladder, but an honest-to-codfish rope ladder, made with a single length of rope and nothing else. It is a very ancient form, yet strangely enough few yachtsmen are familiar with it. As a swimming ladder it is excellent since the rope rungs are large in diameter and comfortable to bare feet.

I would like to suggest another use for it which is strictly my own idea and as far as I know original. Instead of going aloft in a bosun's chair why not use a long rope ladder for an easy climb? It need be only as long as the luff of your mainsail, and when hoisted aloft by the main halliard, with the lower ends secured to the boom or gooseneck, you can quickly reach any part of your spar with little effort. On a recent afternoon I made ten trips to the mainmast head in a bosun's chair on a luff tackle, hoisting myself up and lowering away laboriously. Each time I seemed to gain in weight, and on the last trip I went aloft slowly and came down rather fast, finally collapsing on deck like a ruptured jellyfish. Now had I used one of Smith's Patent Mast Climbers the job would have been easy. Of course there's nothing beats a bosun's chair if you are going aloft to stay awhile, but when you go up to take off a fitting, bring it down to bore a hole, go up and put it back, come down on deck for the tool you forgot to take on the first trip, and so on ad infinitum, it sort of wears you down.

However, you wish to use it, this is an easy ladder to make. First decide how long you want it and the number of steps required, about fifteen inches maximum or twelve inches minimum for spacing. You will need a piece of half inch manila twice as long as the ladder, plus about three feet for each step. Better add a little extra to be sure. Middle the rope and put in a thimble with a stout round seizing. To start the first rung or step, pass

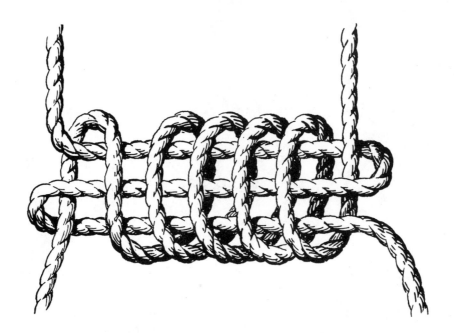

a bight of the left hand leg to the right around the right leg, then pull another bight across to the left. Now take the right hand leg and make seven or eight round turns about the three parts of the two bights just formed and finally pass the end down through the lower bight at the left. The illustration, I think, shows the sequence fairly clearly. Draw the parts up as tight as they will go and you will see that the step just formed is stiff, bulky and just wide enough to fit your instep. While I don't doubt that it could be made wide enough to stand on with both feet, the step would undoubtedly sag to an uncomfortable degree. To the best of my knowledge this ladder has always been made as a "one-footer".

Measure down the left leg for the next step. Again start from the left side with two bights as before, but notice that what is now the left leg was originally the right leg. The reason I call your attention to this is that you thus are expending the same amount of rope in each leg, and when you reach the end of the ladder it comes out even. So always work from the left side.

To finish off the lower end of the ladder you have your choice of several methods. The legs should extend at least twelve inches below the bot-

tom step. They can be finished off with a palm and needle whipping, or a fancy manrope, lanyard or Matthew Walker knot, or the two ends can be short-spliced together to form a loop.

To my mind the most important feature of this ladder is the ease with which it can be stowed. Being made entirely of rope, and not over five or six inches wide at the most, it can actually be coiled down compactly and crammed into almost any shape of compartment. The rope rungs will not loosen or slip and are safer than wooden ones, since your foot is in effect held in a stirrup.

———

To the landsman the language of the sailor must sound like double talk. He knows it is English but it does not make sense. Even the student of etymology would have a tough time trying to trace the origin of such a picturesque term as baggy-wrinkle. Some authorities claim the correct name is railroad sennit, basing their premise on the similarity between railroad tracks and the two strands of marline on which it is woven. Pish, tosh and fiddle-faddle! To a sailor it is *baggywrinkle,* always has been, always will be, and who would argue with a sailor?

Baggywrinkle is a form of chafing gear applied to spars or rigging to

protect sails where constant friction occurs. The most common application is to lazyjacks and topping lifts, where the rubbing of the rope can in time seriously weaken the stitching in the seams and shorten the life of the sails. But to my mind the most important point of application is at the ends of spreaders. When running free, with the boom broad off, the sail presses hard against the unyielding spreader and saws up and down constantly in all but the lightest winds. Here is the place where the most chafe occurs, and here is where most sails are torn or injured. Now the tear is not always due to chafe. Often it is due to the head of the sail sagging off beyond the spreader and catching on it when gybing in heavy weather. Baggywrinkle applied here would certainly eliminate chafe and minimize the danger of the sail fouling the spreader.

All you need is a ball of marline and some old rope. Middle a twelve foot piece of marline, hook it over a nail on your bench or any convenient place that is waist high, and secure the other ends about a foot apart. Now chop up a lot of one-quarter, three-eighths, or half inch rope into pieces about six inches long, and you don't have to be too accurate about the length as they will be trimmed off

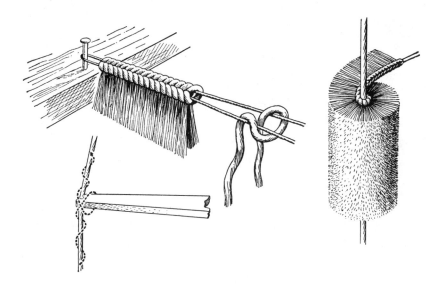

later. Carefully separate the pieces into strands. Stand facing the nail with the marline leading under your right arm. Place a strand crosswise underneath the two strands of marline, bring each end up, over and down through the center, as shown in the illustration. Now grasp both ends of the rope strand with your right hand and pull them strongly away from you towards the nail. Continue by adding strands in like manner. Each strand is jammed close against the preceding one, forming a braid or sennit, with rope strands hanging in a fringe underneath.

When you think you have made enough (a hard thing to estimate) the strands should be unlaid and combed out. Now trim them off with scissors to a uniform length, about one and one-half inches being the customary average. It is applied to the rope or wire by seizing the end in position and winding it spirally the desired distance, where it is again seized.

There are many who object to baggywrinkle on the ground that it is unsightly or that it presents too much wind resistance. If you feel that way there is an excellent substitute. Deep pile sheepskin, cut in one inch strips and wound spirally with the wool side out, works perfectly. On a racing boat I used it for years to cover the spreader tips, and it made a neat job. I have shown a diagram of this application. As to where you can promote a piece of sheepskin, you will have to work that out in your own way. I remember I obtained mine by nonchalantly ripping apart my daughter's sheepskin lined jacket before her horrified eyes. As I said before, you can't argue with a sailor.

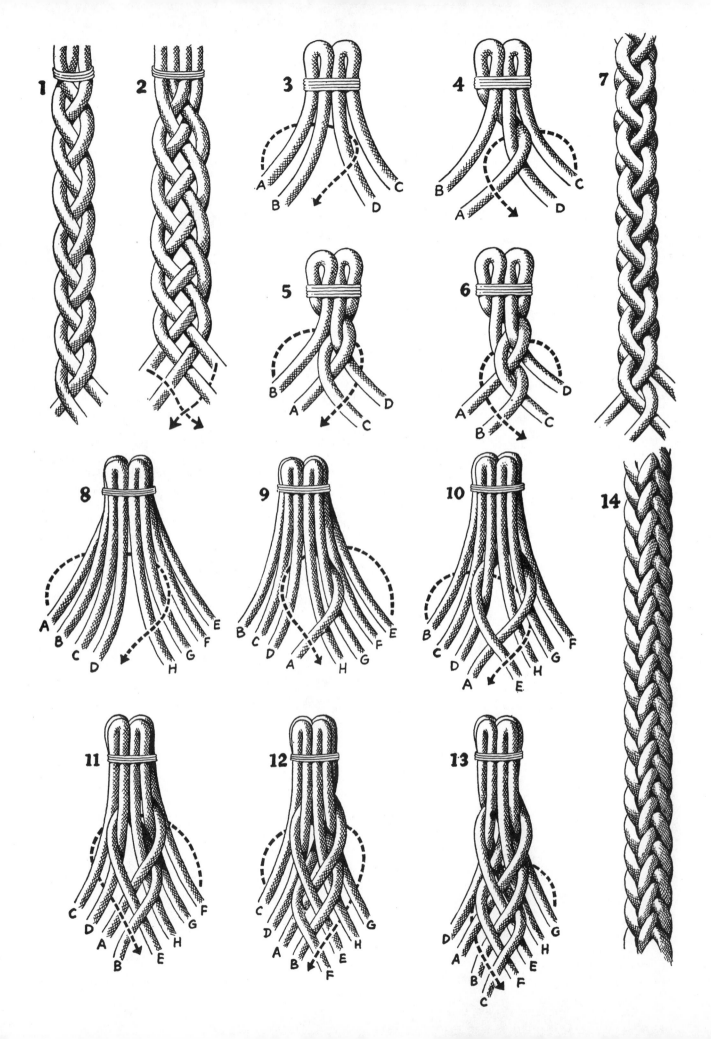

Plaited Sennits

THE plaiting, braiding or weaving of sennit is one of the world's oldest arts, practised by landsman and sailor alike, not for its decorative value alone, but to fill some particular need. In ancient times sennit was a form of rope, and its modern machine made counterpart is found in sashcord, log lines, steam packing and fishing line, to name but a few. In handmade sennits there are literally hundreds of different designs, some useful and others which can only be classed as stunts, however beautiful they may be. A working knowledge of sennit making constitutes one of the basic elements of marlinspike seamanship.

In the days of the square riggers sennits of different kinds were a necessary part of ship's gear, and every sailor worth his salt was expected to know how to make them. Present day yachtsmen will find their use a little more limited, but the need still exists. Lanyards, chest beckets, bell pulls and some forms of rope coverings all require the making of sennits in a variety of styles. With this in mind I have chosen but a few types, all more or less basic, to meet the requirements of the average yachtsman. Used in various combinations, or with minor changes, many different effects can be achieved.

For practice in sennit making I recommend the use of common sashcord, which is actually a machine made sennit. Because of its large diameter it is easy to handle, and the sequence of the passes can be readily followed. Generally speaking, sennit material is small stuff, seine twine or marline.

Illustration 1 shows the familiar three strand flat sennit which every little girl learns when she wears her hair in pigtails. It is hardly necessary to explain how it is done, but examination will not be amiss. Note that each outside strand is passed *over* and in front of the center strand, which lies next to it.

Now look at illustration 2, which is four strand flat sennit. Here the left hand outside strand passes *over* and in front of the adjacent strand, while the right hand outside strand passes *under* and behind its adjacent strand.

Flat sennit can be made with almost any number of strands, but these two will supply the needs of most yachtsmen. Both are greatly improved by using doubled strands, and I suggest you try it. Like all rope work, the strands should be drawn up tightly and evenly to bring out the beauty of form that marks the professional job.

Illustration 7 shows common four strand square sennit. Paradoxical as it may seem, square sennit can also be round. Roll this one under your foot and it becomes smooth and round. Wallop it on all four sides with a mallet and it is definitely square. To make it, seize four strands (or two doubled) at the top and arrange with two strands in either hand. Illustration 3 shows the first move. The top left strand A is passed around back, forward between the right strands C and D, over D and across to the left side again, when it should look like 4. Then the top right strand C is passed around back, forward between B and A, over A and back to the right again, as in 5.

Next the top left strand, which is now B, is passed in back, forward between D and C, and across to the left again when it will look like 6. Then pass the top right strand D around back and forward over B, and back to the right again. This completes the cycle of four passes, and the working ends of all four strands will have assumed their original order of arrangement, as in illustration 3. Now continue by repeating the sequence as before, passing alternately the *top* left and right strands until you have memorized the method, or are sick of the whole thing, or both.

Years ago I sailed a Great South Bay scooter whose jibsheet was a four strand square sennit made of quarter inch cotton sashcord. Since scooters are steered with the jib, the jibsheet is held in the hand, and in a strong breeze the pull is terrific. Plain rope would slip through the hand, so Father solved the problem with square sennit. Once again marlinspike seamanship came to the rescue in the nick of time.

Illustration 14 shows eight strand square sennit, one of the most useful of all sennits. It is firm, handsome, holds its shape well, and stretches very little. The strands are arranged with four in either hand, and the first pass is shown in illustration 8. Strand A, the top left strand, is passed around back, forward under E and F, over G and H, and across to the left again, as shown in 9. Then the top right strand E is passed similarly in back, forward under B and C, over D and A, and back to the right again, as shown in 10. Next top left strand B is passed around back, forward under F and G, over H and E, and across to the left again, as in 11. Illustrations 12 and 13 show the next two passes, F and C. Lack of space prevents showing the two final passes, G and D, which would complete the cycle. The procedure to remember is that the top left and right strands, alternately, are passed across in back to the opposite side, then forward *under two* and *over two* and back to their own sides in front again.

After you have worked a short section of this sennit it is well to go back and take up the slack in each strand, for the success of the job demands that all strands be equally taut and lie fair. Another peculiarity of this sennit is that once you lay it down it is often difficult to remember which strand to start with again.

Since all square sennits are tubular they may be worked around a core, and if more than eight strands are used a core is imperative or the sennit will be flimsy. They can be used as a covering for a stanchion, but generally with doubled or tripled strands, in which case the results will be coachwhipping.

Crown Sennits

CROWN sennits have a character quite different from the plaited sennits described elsewhere. They not only look different but they feel different, for they can be made much firmer, and when the strands are pulled up tightly they do not tend to loosen, but stay put. Hence you can stop anywhere without fear of the sennit's unlaying, and can start it again without wondering where you left off.

Tie a series of crown knots, one on top of another, and you have a crown sennit. It's as simple as that. You can use any number of strands, from three to ten, and get about twenty-four different effects. Because of space limitations, and to save wear and tear on my one good eye, I have illustrated but two. These are basic, and from them all others are evolved.

For the benefit of the uninitiated I have illustrated two crown knots, a right crown and a left crown. There are two types of crown sennit, the alternate and the continuous. The alternate crown sennit is formed by a series of alternate right and left crowns, and the continuous crown sennit consists of a series of identical crowns, which may be either right or left as your fancy dictates. Both types are tubular, which means that they can be made around a core. In fact, if more than six strands are used a core is a necessity, otherwise the sennit would not hold its shape and would lack solidity.

For demonstration I have shown four strand sennits, and we will start with the alternate type, which is also known as Nelson sennit, and therein lies a tale. With Trafalgar and the death of Horatio Nelson the British navy went all out to do honor to its heroic admiral. Many of its present customs and usages were inaugurated in memory of his name, and ever since October 21, 1805, four strand alternate crown sennit has been Nelson sennit to the British tar.

For practice I suggest you use one-eighth inch braided cotton flag halliard. Seize four lengths together and start with a right crown. Note that strand A is passed to the right, behind B, and in front of C. Next strand B is passed *over* the bight of A, behind C and in front of D. Then C is passed over the bight of B and across between D and A. Finally, strand D goes over the bight of C and *through* the bight of A. Draw all the strands up tight and snug. All crown sennits to be successful must be worked as taut as possible or the result will lack firmness.

Now on top of the right crown just tied, work a left crown as shown in the second diagram. Note the passes are the same as in the right crown, but in the opposite direction. After it is drawn up snugly work a right crown again, and continue crowning alternately left and right until the sennit is the length you desire.

Alternate crown   Continuous right crown
sennit   sennit

For a really handsome job, and to demonstrate the possibilities of this sennit, try one using four *doubled* strands, and you will see that the appearance is greatly improved.

The continuous right crown sennit shown should be self explanatory, being merely a series of right crowns.

In appearance it resembles common right-laid rope, and can also be made with doubled strands. If a continuous left crown sennit is desired, tie a series of left crowns, and the result will resemble cable of left-laid rope.

Sennits can also be made in a similar manner by using wall knots, but they stretch abominably and are of no practical value. Therefore I have not shown this.

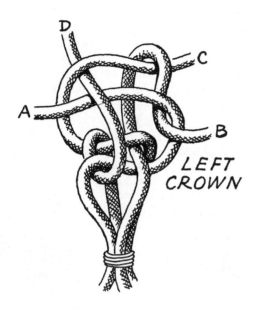

LEFT CROWN

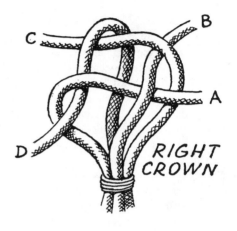

RIGHT CROWN

Rope Handles

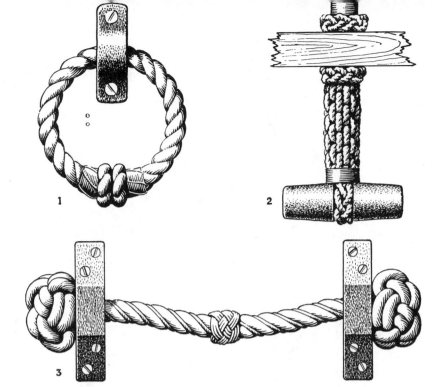

PRACTICAL marlinespike seamanship has its place below deck as well as topside. Not the least important is the making of rope handles for doors, lockers, cupboards and drawers. These give character and individuality to a yacht which cannot be obtained with "store hardware", and they need no brass polish. Furthermore you can paint right over them if you so desire. Personally I like them painted, for it brings out the design and gives them more solidity.

Shown here are three basic types. There are many others, but the purpose of this article is merely to suggest the inherent possibilities and to encourage the individual to use his ingenuity. After all, there are several thousand possible combinations at your command, needing only your creative ability to achieve a pleasing design which will be your own.

Number one is a ring-type handle suitable for almost any door, large or small. A length of ⅜ rope was formed into a grommet about 2½ inches in diameter by joining the ends in a simple shroud knot. Each strand was tucked once, the ends trimmed, and a palm and needle whipping worked on each side of the knot. A wooden cleat was grooved to receive the rope and secured with flat head brass screws countersunk.

A more handsome effect can be had by using four strand rope instead of the three strand shown here, and a more elaborate shroud knot, such as the double diamond, or the four strand double clipper ship. The whipping could be snaked or hitched for added interest.

Number two is a drawer pull which is perhaps a bit more decorative than practical, for it has one fault. It protrudes a bit and might have a tendency to snag clothes or gear if in a passageway. However it is still a good handle and has a nice feel when you grab it.

A wooden toggle was made with a shallow groove around the center. Three long pieces of cod line were seized together near the middle and laid up into a three strand sennet braid just long enough to encircle the toggle. This was seized in place on the toggle, leaving six long lines hanging free. These were then crowned alternately right and left for about two inches where a single diamond knot was made. A hole was bored through the drawer front just large enough to receive the six strands, which were secured by another single diamond on the inside of the drawer. The ends of the strands were then whipped and trimmed close. Another whipping was placed close to the toggle.

Handle number three is for a heavy drawer. It is merely a length of three strand rope, wormed with cod line, and a tack knot worked in each end. A five strand Turk's head decorates the middle of the handle. This makes a really simple job, but it deserves a more elaborate treatment. Your old time sailor would have used four strand rope. He would first unlay it and cover each strand with a piece of old cloth, neatly stitched on. Then he would lay it up again and work up the handle as described. When completely satisfied with its appearance (with due consideration given to the caustic and critical comments of his shipmates) he would shellac the whole thing and give it two coats of white paint. The separate parts of the tack knots would properly and naturally be painted alternately red, white and blue. This would remind him of home, which was a hell of a long way from the God forsaken hole where the old hooker then lay refilling her water casks.

At any rate the result of his labors would be a handsome thing indeed, an authentic sample of an almost lost art that any yachtsman would be glad to own, including the writer of this article.

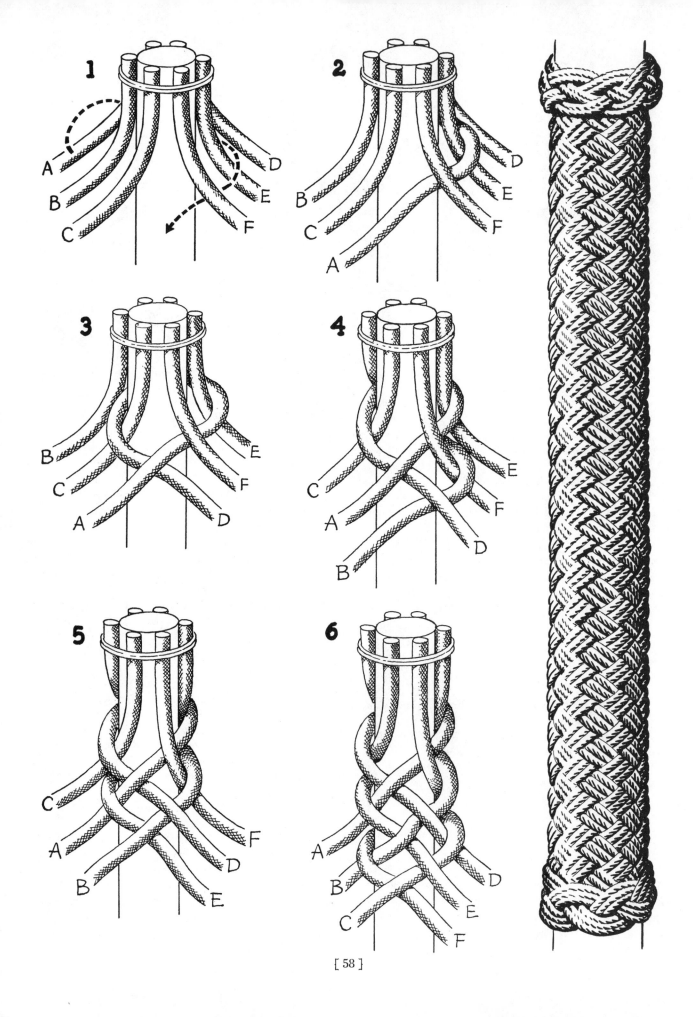

Coachwhipping

WHEN a sailor wishes to apply a covering to a rail, stanchion or handle he has many types of fancy work to choose from, yet invariably coachwhipping is his choice. There are various reasons why this is so. In the first place coachwhipping presents a bold clear design, has a lot of what we call character, and is not at all fussy looking. In fact it is decidedly masculine. It has a nice smooth feel, which is why it is so often used on sea chest beckets, knife handles, bell pulls or any cylindrical object which is grasped by the hand. Finally, it takes less time than other coverings, an important factor when the object to be covered is a long rail or stanchion.

Coachwhipping could rightly be called a number of things. It is a round sennit with a core. It could also be classed as an elongated Turk's head, but the method of working it would be different. The material used in coachwhipping is generally seine twine or fishline, the smaller the diameter of the object the smaller the twine. It is worked with four, six or eight strands. Each strand is composed of two, three, four or five parallel cords or lines.

Four strand coachwhipping, when applied to anything with a diameter greater than one-half inch, does not hide the object completely, but generally leaves diamond shaped interstices between the strands. Because of this objectionable feature I have chosen the six strand type for demonstration. It hides the object completely and is more adaptable.

Before attempting a professional job it is necessary to master the basic method of procedure, and the only way to do this is by practising a simplified method as shown in the six diagrams on the opposite page.

Clamp a twelve inch length of one inch pipe or a broom handle in a vise, vertically. Around the top, equally spaced, seize six lengths of heavy cord as shown in Diagram 1. Separate them into two groups, three out to the left and three to the right. Now pass the left rear strand, A, around in back to the right, and forward between strands D and E, over E and under F, and carry it across to the left side, as the dotted line in Diagram 1 shows. It should now look like Diagram 2.

Next pass the right rear strand, D, around back to the left, forward under B, over C, under A and across to the right. This is shown in Diagram 3.

Now pass the left rear strand, which is now strand B, around back to the right, forward under E, over F, under D and across to the left side again, as shown in Diagram 4.

Next pass the right rear strand E around back to the left and forward, under C, over A, and under B to the right side again as in Diagram 5.

To save space I have combined the next two passes in one drawing, Diagram 6. Pass left rear strand C around to the right, forward under F (which is shown as a right hand strand in Diagram 5), over D, under E, and across to the left. Now pass strand F around back to the left, forward under A, over B, and under C and so to the right.

This completes the cycle of one pass with each of the six strands, but don't let go! Hold the strands in this position while we take another look at the six diagrams and check on our procedure.

Notice that you work alternately, first a left hand strand, then a right hand strand. Each is passed around back to the opposite side, forward under one, over one, under one, and then across in front to its own side again. Now that the first cycle has been completed the strands are all back in their original positions again, A, B and C to the left, D, E and F to the right.

Continue by repeating the procedure as before. When you have completed three cycles, tighten up the whole works and try to arrange the strands so that the design is uniform all the way around. This may seem a bit awkward, but by practice and careful handling it soon becomes easy.

The big trouble we all have is in holding the strands in their respective places and preventing them from getting entangled, particularly when working with multiple strands. For this reason it often helps to have an assistant to pass the strands for you, although I must confess I prefer to do it the hard way, alone.

Want to try four strand coachwhipping? Seize four strands uniformly spaced, pull two out to the left and two to the right. Now proceed with these same diagrams, *but disregard strands C and F entirely.* This is easy, and good practice for you.

Now if you are ready to tackle a real job, such as the six triple strand example I have pictured, measure the length of the coachwhipping you desire and add fifty per cent. That will give you the length of the strands. If you want twelve inches of covering the cords should be at least eighteen inches long. Wind each group of three cords about your fingers in the form of a small coil and snap a rubber band around each coil. This should keep them from tangling. It probably won't, but it helps. Narrow Turk's head knots or a snaked whipping are generally applied at the ends of the coachwhipping in order to hide the seized ends. One last important tip. Once you start, don't stop, for if you lay it down and come back to it later you will find it difficult to determine which strand goes where.

Grafting, Pointing and Hitching

IN THIS series of articles on the more decorative applications of marlinspike seamanship it is only natural that some will question their practical value, particularly relative to the needs of present day yachtsmen. "It may have been hot stuff back in the days of the square riggers, but of what value is it aboard my twenty-four footer?" they'll ask. Well, those members of our fraternity who feel they must go to sea with Venetian blinds and chromium windshield wipers may be a bit hard to convince, but it is still my contention that regardless of the size or type of yacht, be it sail or power, there are many places where the judicious application of a bit of fancywork is not only fitting and proper, but very practical as well.

Needle hitching on a screwdriver handle is still the best way to keep a greasy hand from slipping, and a coachwhipped stanchion needs no brass polish. Even if you are utterly barren of original ideas, a Turk's head knot on a toothbrush handle will definitely identify it as yours. But aside from all this, once accomplished you will have put something of yourself into your yacht which forever sets her apart and gives her a personality and character different from that of every other vessel, including that tub lying at the next mooring.

The ketch Morning Star is a centerboarder, and the centerboard pennant runs in a brass tube which extends from the top of the case vertically to the cabin roof. This gives support to the roof and serves as an excellent handhold in a seaway. Being allergic to work, I have never polished that brass pipe and I don't intend to, but some day I intend to cover it with grafting and coachwhipping, separated by Turk's heads. It's a job I've been saving for a rainy day when we're cooped up below with nothing to do. Here, if ever, marlinspike art is going to be the means of salvaging an otherwise wasted day.

A word about the illustrations might not be amiss. They were drawn for one purpose only—to show as clearly as possible the methods by which certain textures are achieved. This meant abandoning photographic realism for the sake of clarity. Therefore it should be emphasized that the finished product is far more beautiful than the drawings indicate, and the work itself is easier to do than to portray.

Grafting, also known as Spanish hitching, is the sailor's common method of covering an object in a rather plain manner. It is generally applied to sea chest beckets, rope handles or stanchions. Its texture is fairly smooth, and can be varied at will in two ways. The finer the twine you use, the smoother the texture. Increasing the tension of the parts also improves the effect. While there is no rule regarding grafting I would confine its use to objects under an inch and a half in diameter.

Grafting consists of numerous strands of fine fishline known as fillers hitched continuously about a spirally wound line called the warp. The warp will be at least thirty times the length of the fillers, and if possible should be considerably stiffer. Tarred Cuttyhunk makes an excellent warp. A number of filler strands are cow-hitched to one end of the warp, fairly close together and of sufficient number to just encircle the object to be covered. Secure it in position with the working or free end of the warp leading to the left. Hold the warp in the left hand, and as you wind it around the object clockwise hitch each filler strand to it in turn with the right hand. At all times the warp must be held taut so it will not distort or capsize. Draw the hitches up snugly or the texture will be irregular. Whether you choose the underhand form or the overhand, the procedure is the same but the textures are different. Of the two overhand grafting is by far the handsomer, being much smoother and slicker. When shellacked and painted it looks very much like snakeskin.

Pointing is just another form of grafting, or vice versa, except that the hitches in this case are taken about the fillers with the warp. The fillers are single strands which are evenly spaced about the object and seized in position, and the lower ends are likewise seized. Needless to say the filler strands should be as taut as possible. Pointing was originally used for covering the end of a rope which had been tapered to a point for easier reeving, but for our use it is reserved for covering an object of rather large diameter, such as a fender.

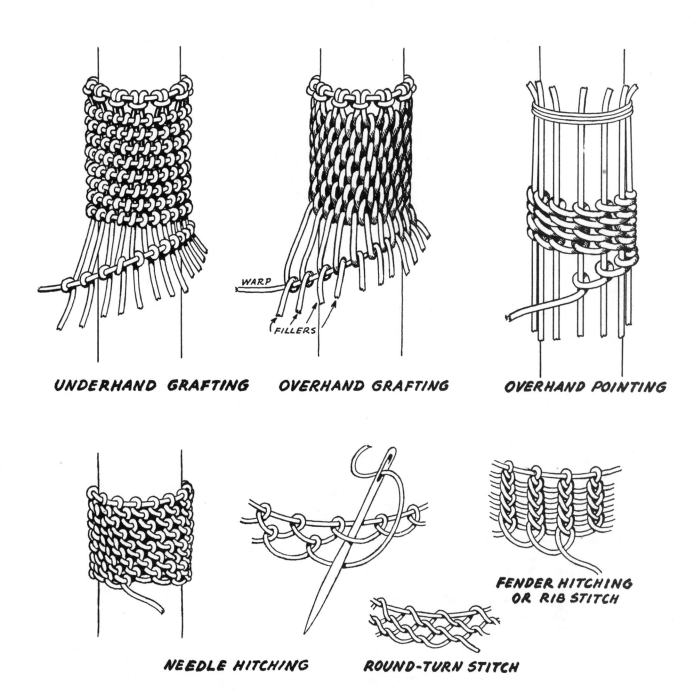

UNDERHAND GRAFTING　　**OVERHAND GRAFTING**　　**OVERHAND POINTING**

WARP

FILLERS

NEEDLE HITCHING　　**ROUND-TURN STITCH**

FENDER HITCHING OR RIB STITCH

Grafting and pointing are very easy to work, and build rather rapidly. While it looks like a somewhat monotonous procedure, it is so interesting to watch the texture develop that you are rarely bored. If the object to be covered is rather long, such as a stanchion, don't make the mistake of applying grafting the entire length. Vary the design by covering a section in the center with coachwhipping, and cover the joints with Turk's heads. As you acquire a working knowledge of the basic elements of decorative rope work you learn to combine them in any number of ways, the variety of which is dependent only on your ingenuity, as your fancy dictates.

Needle hitching is the most useful of all coverings and the fastest to work. It is adaptable to almost any shape, spherical or cylindrical. As its name implies, it is worked with a sail needle. Its texture gives a nonskid surface to any tool having a handle, such as a sheath knife, screwdriver or icepick. Due to its more open texture it makes a better covering for a tiller end than the usual serving of marline and perspiration will not make it slippery. Applied to the lower half of a drinking glass and shellacked, it makes a perfect holder for frosty drinks.

Thread a long piece of fine fishline in a sail needle and tie the end rather loosely about the object. Then put on a series of loose hitches all around. Next start a second round of hitches, but this time put them on the loops formed by the first series, and proceed ad infinitum. Experience will teach you how tight to pull and how close the hitches should be, but be sure they are uniformly spaced or you will louse up the whole works.

In the diagram I have shown the hitches being applied from left to right, but if it is easier for you to work from right to left the result will be about the same. If the object to be covered tapers, omit a hitch at regular intervals. If the diameter progressively increases, merely add an extra hitch or two each time around.

The round turn stitch is even simpler and should require no explanation. Here the strand is not hitched, but looped around and around. It gives a smoother texture and should be drawn up rather snugly.

Fender hitching gives a ribbed effect almost identical with the knitting of your sweater, and for covering a water jug it can't be beat. The ribs can be as close as your fancy dictates. It is started the same as needle hitching, but successive hitches are taken about the neck of each hitch in the preceding row instead of on the bights. For a professional appearance keep the hitches perfectly aligned and evenly spaced.

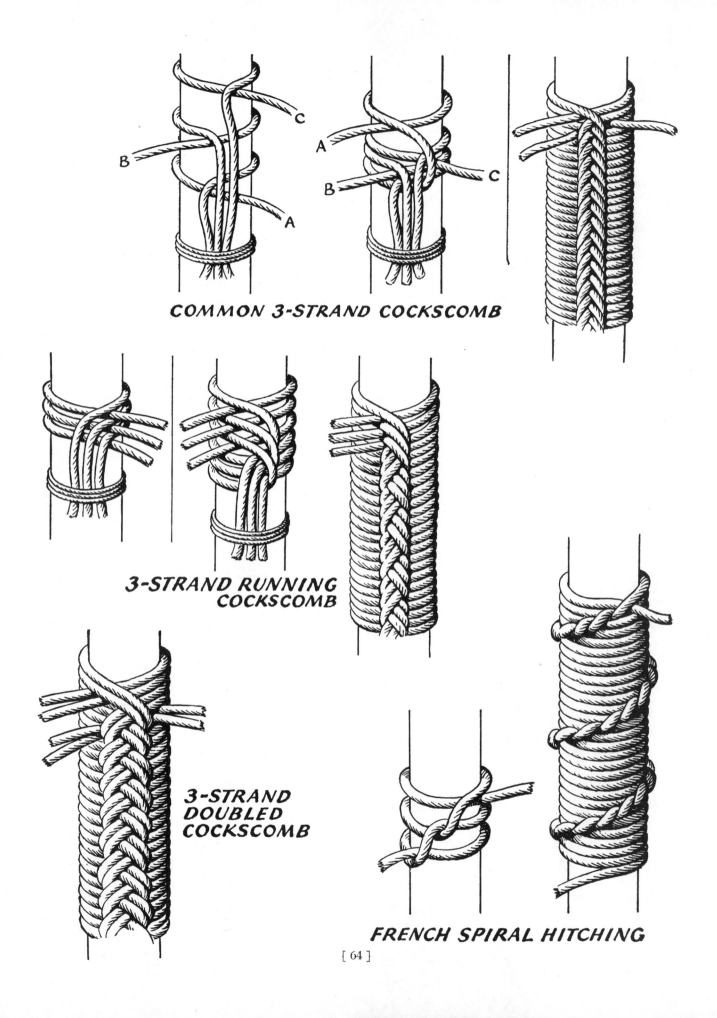

COMMON 3-STRAND COCKSCOMB

3-STRAND RUNNING COCKSCOMB

3-STRAND DOUBLED COCKSCOMB

FRENCH SPIRAL HITCHING

Cockscombing

THE art of rope work is so ancient that nomenclature is ofttimes a problem. I like the name cockscombing because it is picturesque, but it would be equally correct to call it ringbolt hitching or even kackling. Originally it was chafing gear or a covering applied to iron rings, the ringbolts which ranged along the decks or the anchor rings. It can be used to cover any round object such as a stanchion or hand rail, but its best application by far is the covering of the eyes in sea chest beckets, which is the reason I am showing it.

Cockscombing consists of nothing more than a series of half hitches made with from one to six strands of white cord, the resultant design being achieved by varying the number of strands and the direction of the hitches. The first design I have illustrated is the most commonly used, the ordinary three strand cockscomb. Seize three cords to the object to be covered. Now bring up the first strand, A, and form a righthand half hitch. Bring up the next strand, B, and form a lefthand half hitch above the first. Then bring up the third strand, C, and form a righthand half hitch above all. This completes the first cycle.

Now bring up strand A again and make another half hitch, this time to the *left*. Continue by half hitching each strand in turn, alternately right and left. Draw the hitches up snugly each time and keep them aligned. This results in a raised braid design, and if it is an eye that is being covered the design would of course be on the outer circumference of the eye.

The next design shown is the three strand running cockscomb. Three strands are seized as before, and each strand is half hitched to the right. Then all three are half hitched to the left. Keep all the hitches together, and continue with three to the right and three to the left alternately.

The three strand double cockscomb hardly needs any description, as it is made exactly the same as the first one shown except that doubled strands are used. The design however is more interesting.

After you have made and memorized these three basic designs I suggest you experiment a bit. Try one with, say, five strands, or perhaps four strands doubled, and notice how the design varies in form and texture. By experimenting on your own, and inventing, you will learn much more about ropework than you would by carefully copying specific instructions.

The last design shown, one strand French hitching, is not a cockscomb, and is not suitable for chest beckets or similar objects. It is, however, an excellent covering for a rail, stanchion or pipe, particularly if it has considerable length. It is made by half hitching one strand continuously to the right in a spiral. Keep the hitches tight and uniform. Each end of French hitching is generally covered by a Turk's head knot to finish it off. As an alternate to this design try it with a double strand and note the difference.

The SEA CHEST

WITH the passing of what is known as the Glorious Era of Sail there came to an end an ancient custom—the use of the sea chest by the sailor. From time immemorial men roamed the seven seas with their belongings stowed in the picturesque and often beautiful chest that became the mark of their calling. Rarely permitted in the naval service, often seen in the merchantmen, the sea chest was always carried in the whalers. With the cessation of whaling the chest was no longer needed, and the custom died quietly and abruptly.

Today an occasional specimen turns up in an old barn or attic, whereupon it suddenly acquires a value that would astound its former owner were he still living. This is as it should be, for it represents an era and a breed of man long since gone, and an art that would be lost to posterity but for the interest of today's yachtsmen. The purpose of these articles is to remind these yachtsmen of the heritage that is theirs, of the opportunity they have to perpetuate the traditions, customs and skills of that era to which they owe so much.

The sea chest was the sailor's wardrobe, his secret hiding place, his hope chest, the repository of his pitifully few treasures, his one bit of privacy where privacy was almost nonexistent.

Except for the cheap affairs with castiron beckets sold by the outfitters he invariably made his own, and no two sailors made them alike. Weeks and months of odd moments went into the making of the rope beckets, for they were the culmination of all that he had learned of his craft. In fact chest beckets represent the highest type of marlinespike seamanship. I have seen some that in my opinion rank as works of art. At least they come nearer to it than some of the monstrosities presented as "art" by our galleries. Having examined many old beckets and dissected some that were rotten with age, I never cease to marvel at the infinite care, the countless hours

and the effort toward perfection that went into their making. Truly some of those sailors of old were artists.

Chests varied greatly in size. Some were so small that they were in fact ditty boxes, and some were so large as to appear impractical. The average length was about 36 inches, light enough for ease in handling and small enough for a crowded forecastle. Some had slanted fronts and backs, a few had short legs, most had a framing piece around the bottom to keep them off the deck. The corners were always dovetailed, and the sides, bottom and top were of a single plank, usually about ¾ of an inch thick. Americans generally used white pine, but I have seen them made of mahogany, sandalwood, cedar, teak and foreign woods classed as rare. Usually a ditty box with lid was built in at one end just below the top edge. All had locks, but padlocks were rare.

Most chests were painted very plainly outside—a quiet green, gray or blue. If decoration was desired it was generally used on the inside of the lid. Stars, rope, knots, anchors, mermaids, ships, or the owners' names were popular motifs. But the beckets were the dominant decorative note. The chest's plain exterior only emphasized the design of the handles.

So much for description. Now how about making one for yourself? Granted you may not be shipping out very soon in a whaling bark, but there's nothing like being prepared. Anyhow a sea chest is a swell place to store sails, and if you have no sails, blankets. It's an extra seat or coffee table for the living room. Or you could make one just for the hell of it!

A friend of mine has often expressed a desire to own some day a cruiser large enough to accommodate a sea chest. To him and others similarly minded may I suggest making a miniature edition and using it as a ditty box. Capt. Tom Crosby of Sayville, New York, came home in 1852 from a three year Pacific cruise in the

sure to make it as tight and firm as you can, then secure it by hitching with marline.

Now cover each eye with 3 strand coxcombing—3 strands of small white cord laid up into alternate half hitches, first to the right and then to the left. When the eyes are covered down to the throats, seize the ends of the cords to the rope proper.

A sufficient number of strands of cod line to cover the rope are seized just below the eyes, and outside Spanish hitching is worked for a distance of about 4¼ inches from each eye, where the ends are again seized. The remainder of the becket, which is the part grasped with the hand, is covered with 4 strand coachwhipping, also of white cod line.

Now go back over the work you have done so far. See that every strand has equal tension, every part is tight and snug and uniformly laid. If not, take up the slack in the offending strand, and above all else *take your time.* This is slow work, and a perfect job will take many hours. I have spent over three weeks on a pair of beckets, working evenings.

When satisfied that you cannot improve it, finish it up by working the Turk's head knots as shown, a 3 strand knot next to the eyes and a 5 strand knot covering the juncture of the Spanish hitching and the coachwhipping.

You are now ready for the bolt, the part which holds the bail or handle to the cleat. Put two tight seizings in the center of a 4 foot piece of ½ inch rope, about 4 or 4½ inches apart. After whipping the strands unlay one end of the rope to the seizing. Each strand must now be covered with light sailcloth or cotton drill. Cut the material in strips the proper width and stitch it on with heavy sewing cotton, such as button thread. Be sure the stitching follows a straight line down the strand on what would be the center of the rope. Do not follow the lay of the rope. Unlaying the strands slightly will help in this respect.

When all three strands are covered, make them up into a manrope knot, doubled. The trick here is to keep the stitching hidden, and finally to take out every bit of slack so the knot will be as firm and hard as you can make it.

The center of the bolt between the seizings is now covered with leather stitched in place. This leather, which is about 1/16 inch thick, protects the parts from chafing.

Next make two leather washers with saw-toothed or pinked edges, ⅛ inch thick and the same diameter as the manrope knot you have just made. The hole should be just big enough to admit the leathered bolt.

To assemble your becket, first slip a washer on the bolt next to the manrope knot, then both eyes of the bail, and finally the other washer. Now proceed to cover the remaining 3 strands of the rope and tie the other knot.

Spread the legs of the bail apart as far as they will go and measure the distance between. This will be the width to make your cleat. Tie the legs of the bail to-

whaling bark Congaree with a beautiful sea chest less than twenty inches long which held his scrimshaw tools, palm, needle case, marlinespikes, serving mallets and fids.

You always make the beckets first and the chest last, not only because the beckets are the most interesting part of the work, but by the time they are finished the chest will furnish a welcome change of pace.

Take a length of ⅜ inch rope and make a small eye splice (about ⅞ inch inside diameter) in each end as shown in the drawing. Next build up a mouse or "puddening" of canvas to shape the handle as shown, thick in the middle and tapering evenly down to the eyes. Be

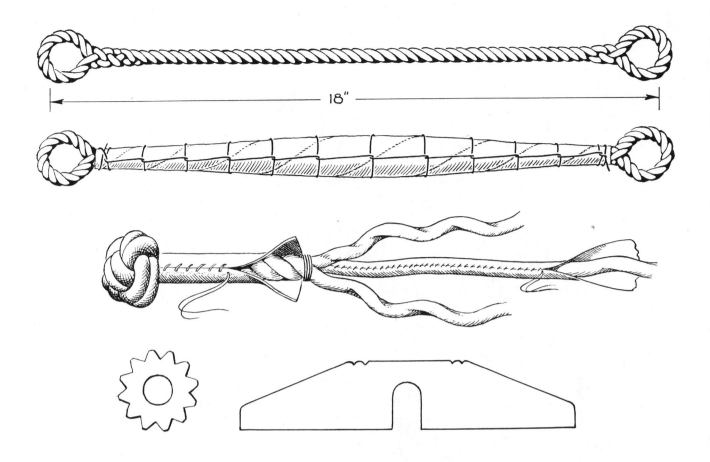

gether and pull the leather washers away from the knots. Give the knots a coat of shellac and two or three coats of paint—one pair of strands red, the next pair white, and the other one blue.

While this is drying make your cleat. This will be about 10 inches long of oak or white pine, and carved to suit your fancy. It should be painted to match the chest and secured with rivets, not screws.

Well, there you have a finished becket, and all that remains is to make a mate for it and a chest of your own designing. Actually both beckets should be made at once, alternating from one to the other as you proceed step by step. When your chest is entirely completed don't forget that one thing still has to be added—the smell! So toss in a brand new ball of tarred marline for that ambrosial fragrance God gave to true sailors.

If this article has resulted in your turning out a reasonably creditable job (as is my earnest hope) I can guarantee two things—you will be (1) tired, and (2) fully entitled to your degree of B.A.—Becket Artist.

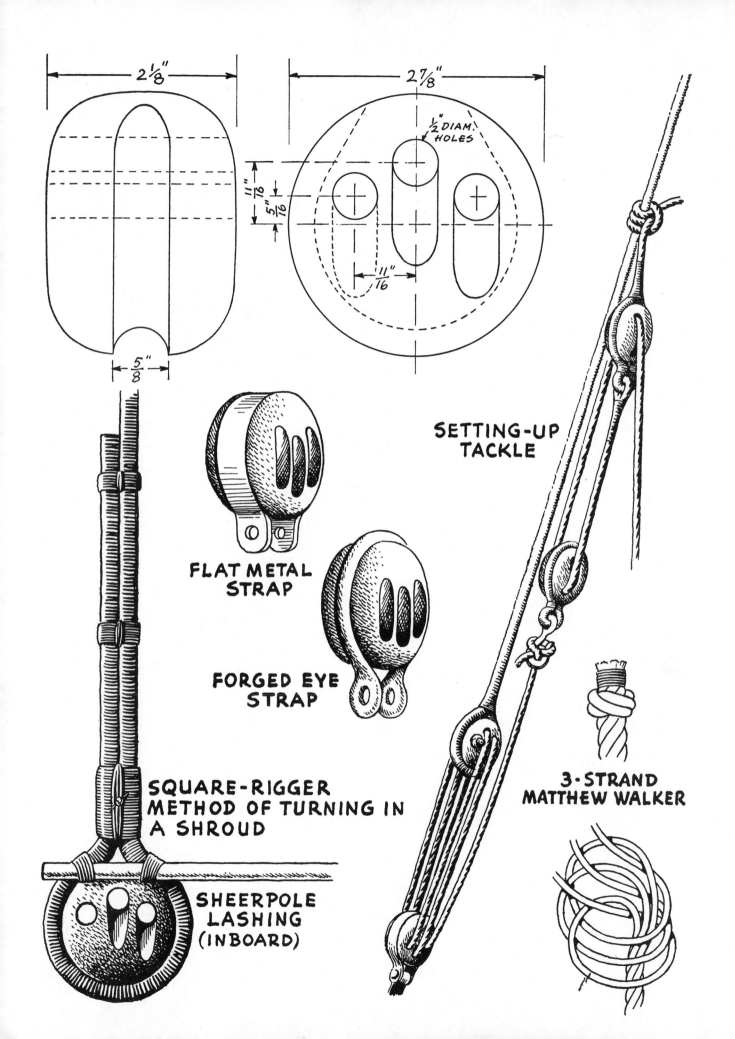

2 1/8"

2 7/8"

1/2" DIAM. HOLES

11/16"
5/16"

11/16"

5/8"

SETTING-UP
TACKLE

FLAT METAL
STRAP

FORGED EYE
STRAP

SQUARE-RIGGER
METHOD OF TURNING IN
A SHROUD

SHEERPOLE
LASHING
(INBOARD)

3·STRAND
MATTHEW WALKER

Deadeyes and Lanyards

REVERTING to a rigging detail usually associated with a by-gone era is generally done, I suspect, for sentimental reasons, but deadeyes and lanyards are entirely practical today. On gaff rigged yachts they are resilient, easy on the spars and rigging, and their elasticity is quite noticeable. They give under sudden strains and bad weather, and in times of stress (God forbid!) are quickly cut away. Most objections to their use by the uninformed stem from a mistaken idea that lanyards stretch abominably. This is definitely not so. New lanyards when first set up will take a month or so of sailing to get the stretch out, but after that they are quite stable *provided they are properly tarred.* Keep the weather out and you will have no trouble.

Deadeyes and lanyards are seen but seldom nowadays, having been supplanted by the more easily obtained turnbuckles. Deadeyes have long since disappeared from the marine hardware catalogues and are obtainable only on special order, if at all. Yachtsmen wishing to convert to the old fashioned rig will probably make their own, in which case something more than a photograph of an old square rigger will be needed. The purpose of this article is to endeavor to supply some of the needed information.

Lignum vitae has for over a hundred years been the accepted material for deadeyes, and prior to that elm was considered first choice. Walnut, locust and hickory have also been used successfully. Whichever is chosen, the wood must be tough, dense, close grained and well seasoned, with no tendency to check. Cooking the deadeyes in hot linseed oil for several hours will help prevent checking and make them weatherproof.

On the opposite page are measured drawings of the upper deadeyes from a thirty-two foot oyster sloop, deceased. Their proportions are typical. Notice that the left hole, at the inboard side where the lanyard knot is tied, is left sharp edged, but elsewhere the holes are faired or softened by means of a groove cut with a gouge. Notice also the groove in the edge of the deadeye to take the parceled and served wire shroud. In the example shown the shrouds were three-eighths inch galvanized iron.

There are several ways to turn in the shrouds. They may be spliced around the deadeye as shown here, or the square rigger method of a large round seizing and two flat seizings may be used. Another way is to put a thimble splice in the end of the shroud, and by using a strap identical with the one on the lower deadeye, it may be bolted to the upper deadeye.

The lower deadeyes must be strapped to receive the chainplates. Store bought deadeyes come grooved to take a round strap with forged eyes, but a flat strap can be bent and bored for the bolt more easily and cheaply. The chainplate can be bent to form an eye and riveted or brazed.

[71]

Lanyards should be three strand tarred Italian hemp, the same diameter as the wire shroud, and can be obtained from any sailmaker. The lanyard knot may be a three strand Matthew Walker, the strands laid up and seized at the top as shown. Lanyards are always rove right handed, as rope is coiled, with the knot placed at the inboard side of the left hand hole of the upper deadeye. This brings the knots on the forward side of the starboard deadeyes, and the after side of the port deadeyes. When the working end of the lanyard has been rove through the last hole (right side of lower deadeye),

it is brought up and cow hitched to the shroud, and the end is brought down and seized three times between two standing parts, as I have shown in the first illustration.

Setting up the rigging is simple. A tackle (single purchase will do) is secured to the shroud as high as you can reach with a rolling hitch. The lanyard and the holes in the deadeyes are well greased and the lanyard is bent to the hook of the lower block with a becket hitch. Haul away on your tackle until the shroud has the desired tension and hold your gain while a helper seizes (temporarily) the standing parts of the lan-

yard together. Then cast off from your tackle and secure the lanyard end as previously described.

Where there is more than one shroud to a side, sheer poles are lashed inboard of the upper deadeyes as shown. They may be made of half inch galvanized iron rod, painted black, and served to align the deadeyes. Then tie the whole assembly together.

When all has been lined up satisfactorily the lanyards should be well tarred for weather protection, and retarred yearly. Lanyards so treated and well cared for will be good for many years of service, getting stiffer as they age, but none the less strong.

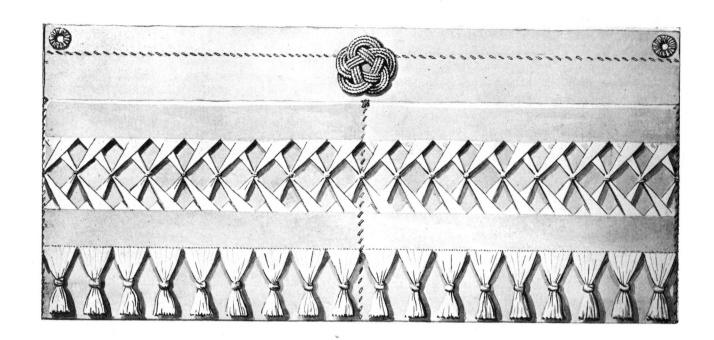

Decorative Wall Bag

A Bit of Fancywork From a Whaler

ONE of the lost arts of the old time sailorman is the making of drawnwork and fringes in canvas. The horizontal filler threads are withdrawn in sections and the remaining vertical warps are tied or woven together into intricate designs and fringes, thus giving a pleasing decorative effect to an otherwise plain and uninteresting piece of canvaswork.

In the days of the whaleships the whale lines were protected from the weather when not in use by canvas covers fitted over the line tubs which were worked into intricate drawnwork designs and finished off with fancy fringes round about. In a like manner the whaleman decorated the canvas cover of his sea chest, up in the forecastle. In fact, almost anything requiring a canvas cover was apt to be ornamented in some fashion by the marlinspike sailor.

Wall bags, such as I have shown here, were very common in olden times, often made for the wife or sweetheart back in God's country. I recollect seeing one as a boy adorning the kitchen wall in an old farmhouse, and serving as a filing case for the housewife's treasured recipes. It occurred to me that some yachtsman might want to make one to hang on his cabin bulkhead. In it

he could stow his pipes, spare socks or false teeth, and he could point with pride to another example of his sea-going handiwork.

The example illustrated measures 8 by 18 inches and has two pockets. It requires a piece of 8 or 10 ounce canvas 18 inches wide by about 16 deep. First, fold the top edge over back to form a 1 inch hem and flat-seam it with waxed doubled sail twine. In each end of the hem make a worked eyelet by punching a hole and sewing a grommet of marline over it with a buttonhole stitch.

Draw a pencil line across the canvas 8 inches down from the top, and fold the bottom up on this line. Sew the two edges together with a round seam 6 inches up from the fold. This leaves a flap hanging down in which the design is worked.

The crossthreads or fillers are withdrawn from a section 2½ inches deep, starting 1 inch from the top edge of the flap. This is best done by picking up a thread in the center with an awl or sail needle and pulling it out from both sides simultaneously. When finished you have a 2½ inch band across the canvas consisting of vertical threads only. These are divided into half inch groups, and should be ticked off with a pencil.

Starting at the left, gather up the first and fourth group and seize them together in the center with a single yarn or thread, passing the first behind the second and the fourth in front of the third. The second group is seized to the edge of the canvas. Now seize the third and sixth groups in a like manner and continue across the cloth.

One inch below start withdrawing the remainder of the crossthreads to form the fringe. Half-knots are tied in each one inch group of warps and the tassels are trimmed off evenly. Now sew all three thicknesses of canvas together down the center, thus making the two pockets.

Make a three strand, five bight flat Turk's head, or any other decorative flat knot, and sew it to the upper center with hidden stitches. This completes the job, and with two brass cup hooks it's ready to hang up.

If there are any yachtsmen who might hesitate to make drawnwork for fear of being called sissies, I would remind them that many a horny handed tough son of a sea cook turned out work of this type that would put the East Jonesville Ladies' Sewing Club to shame.

Tom Crosby's *Ditty Box*

Capt. Thomas L. Crosby

IN THE article on sea chests which appears on page 67 I suggested that yachtsmen who desired a sea chest but lacked the necessary stowage space might well consider making a miniature chest for use as a ditty box.

Thomas L. Crosby was quite a man. Born in Osterville, Massachusetts, in 1834, he settled in Sayville, New York, at the close of the Civil War where he died in 1907.

At the ripe old age of nine Tom Crosby went to sea as cook in his father's coasting schooner. At fourteen he received his papers declaring to all and sundry that he was an able bodied seaman. But he had a yearning for far places and distant seas, so he shipped out of New Bedford in the bark Congaree, bound for the Pacific on a three year whaling cruise. This last was a joker, for Tom was gone from home a full ten years, and the Congaree forever. The old ship's bones lie on the bottom of the sea somewhere off the coast of Chile. At the close of the Civil War he acquired a wife and the command of a neat little coaster, the Doctor Powers. After a succession of good, bad or indifferent vessels he bought the three master Mary B. Wellington, one of the handsomest schooners ever built, and perhaps the last to carry a full length figurehead. She was his pride and joy, and in her he sailed until his death.

But what has all this to do with sea chests? Well, for one thing I never see a sea chest without thinking of Tom Crosby. All his life he carried with him through fair weather and foul a miniature sea chest, his ditty box, which reposes here beside me as I write. He had the hands and heart of an artist, as did so many of the sailors in his time, and many were the beautiful articles he wrought for loved ones back home. Be it rope, wood or bone, he was a master in his craft. Truly the art of marlinespike seamanship owes much to sailors such as he.

A few years ago I undertook the repair of a beautiful mahogany sewing box he had made for his daughter. Elaborately inlaid with ebony, lemonwood and pearl shells, it had me stymied for a while, for some of the inlays were missing. But under a layer of dust and cobwebs in the old woodshed we found his ditty box, filled with a wondrous collection of curious handmade tools and many scraps of material left over from the making of this very sewing box way back in 1852. There was whale ivory, bone and baleen, patterns for inlays, partly finished trinkets and scrimshaw work. But it was the ditty box itself that held my interest.

Made of half inch white pine, it was painted a dull apple green. The rope handle was of exquisite workmanship, and an exact duplicate of one shown in Clifford Ashley's book of knots from the whaler Acushnet.

While sea chests are fairly common, being carried by most all sailors in the old days, it is an interesting but not very well known fact that miniature chests were often used to hold ships' papers.

I think the drawings are sufficiently clear to enable anyone to build a duplicate of this chest should he desire, but the handle deserves some explanation. A grommet three inches in diameter was laid up with quarter inch hemp rope. A white cloth cover was then stitched on, the tiny stitches being taken on the inside edge of the grommet. It was then wormed all around with fine white cord. The upper third of the becket was protected from chafe by a stitched-on covering of fine leather, apparently goat or kidskin, and the ends were pinked. Two three-strand Turk's head knots of fine fishline finished the job, and the cleat was secured to the chest with four handmade nails, clinched on the inside.

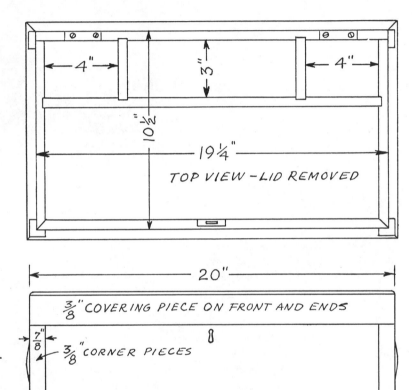

4"   3"   4"

10½"

19¼"

TOP VIEW — LID REMOVED

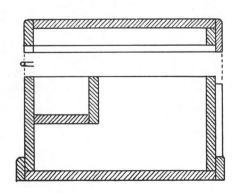

10⅞"

1¾"   ¾"

4"

½"

7¼"

END

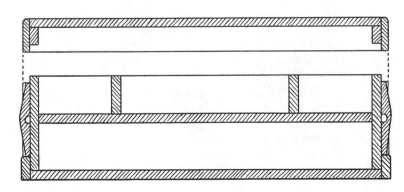

20"

⅜" COVERING PIECE ON FRONT AND ENDS

⅞"

⅜" CORNER PIECES

½" FRAMING PIECE ALL AROUND

FRONT

The Rigger's Little Helper

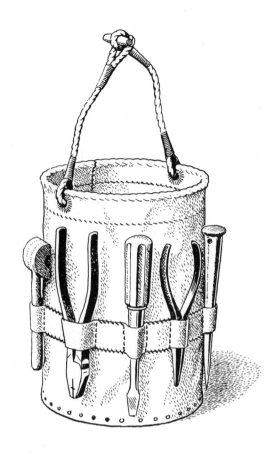

LIKE the proverbial plumber's helper I have for years suffered from forgetfulness in the matter of tools. In fact I've probably made more round trips between masthead and deck to retrieve forgotten tools than anybody on the Great South Bay. For the first ten years or so it is just a little annoying, and during the next ten years you think that perhaps you ought to do something about it. Finally, when old Father Time can no longer be ignored, you realize that one trip a day is about all you can handle and still call it fun.

I think one reason for my forgetfulness has been a lack of means to carry enough tools for unforeseen needs. It was my practice to load all four pockets of my dungarees, and the overflow went in my shirt, if any. That this was highly impractical never occurred to me until that fateful morning last summer. Right across from the town dock, in full view of the embarking multitude, I made the mistake of standing up in the bosun's chair while at the masthead. As I carefully drew myself erect I lost my pants, ballasted as they were with an assortment of heavy hardware. The attendant embarrassment was bad enough, but I found myself faced with the seemingly impossible trick of holding on with one hand and retrieving my pants with the other, the while balancing myself precariously on the wobbling bosun's chair. Fortunately the wind was in the east and I could not hear the comments of the spectators, but when I was safely on deck once more I did not stop to take a bow, having a sudden desire to be alone.

Out of that experience came the idea for this handy little bucket, a portable container for all the gear of a marlinspike sailor. Inside go the balls of marline and sail twine, the coil of serving wire, spare shackles and cotter pins, friction tape and tubes of cement and grease. Round about the outside are the tools, each held in a loop made to fit and in plain sight. Notice the toggle-and-becket bail. That makes it easy to secure the bucket to the southeast leg of the bosun's chair.

Observe the rope grommet enclosed in the seam around the top. This means that the mouth will always stay open, with everything inside accessible and in plain sight.

I assume the illustration is sufficiently clear to enable anyone to make the bucket without detailed drawings and diagrams. The diameter is 7 inches and the height 9 inches. This calls for a piece of 8 to 12 ounce canvas roughly 11 by 24 inches. The bottom is a 7 inch disk of half inch pine, mahogany or plywood. Place the canvas in position around the bottom and mark the size with a pencil, allowing a 1 inch seam with the raw edges turned in. Now remove it and sew with a flat seam stitch. Turn the lower edge under ½ inch and work it carefully onto the bottom, then fasten with ⅜ inch copper tacks spaced 1 inch apart.

Take a single strand of ⅜ inch rope 69 inches long and lay it up into a grommet 7 inches in diameter. A simpler though not so professional grommet can be made by taking a 28 inch piece of rope and short splicing the ends together. Placing the grommet inside the top, turn down the canvas for a 1½ inch seam and flat seam it. Two eyelets are worked in this seam close under the grommet to take the bail.

Your favorite tools are held in place by a 1½ inch strap, sewn securely between the loops with double sail twine, well waxed. Extreme care should be taken that the loop fits the tool, and that the tool does not extend below the bottom of the bucket, else it would unship when the bucket is set down on the deck.

The two legs of the bail are of ¼ inch rope spliced in and served. One terminates in a spliced-in toggle and the other in a small eye splice. Now load up your bucket, toggle it onto your bosun's chair, and you are ready to go aloft. But for heaven's sake, be sure your pants are well secured.

Wooden Bilge Pumps

AFTER two days and nights of easterly gales and torrential rains, the morning dawned with clearing skies and the meadows sparkled in the welcome sunshine as I walked down the path to the creek to see how the boat had fared. It was the sort of morning that made one glad to be alive and anxious to be up and doing. I found my rowboat half full of rainwater, and then it dawned on me that my bilge pump was aboard the Filibuster on the other side of the creek. As I debated the question of whether to go back to the house for a bailer I heard a familiar homely sound. In the sun drenched doorway of his shanty, his ancient straw hat cocked jauntily over one eye, sat "Uncle" Bob Smith, playing "Silver Threads among the Gold" on a lilac leaf.

Being a true lover of the arts, I waited until he had finished his opus, spat out the lilac leaf and replaced it with a mouthful of Union Leader, and then asked if I might borrow a bilge pump. He reached inside and handed out a battered old wooden affair, the likes of which I had never seen before. It was made of half inch cedar, about 4 feet long and 4 inches square. As I pulled out the plunger to see how it was constructed Bob said, "Never seen one of them before, did you? Lots of them around when I was a boy. They don't make no noise, 'n they don't chew up the plankin' like them tin ones do." As an afterthought he added, "Don't cost nothin' neither."

The construction of the pump was simplicity itself. The plunger consisted of a 3 inch square of sole leather tacked to a 2 inch square block of wood, with a 1 inch oak handle. The valve was a plug of wood in the bottom of the pump, with a 2 inch hole in it covered by a leather flap tacked over it.

The pump raised an enormous stream of water, and after a lifetime familiarity with all sorts of metal pumps I was struck by its quietness. There was none of the screeching, scraping, rusty clatter I had always known, and for the first time in my life I enjoyed pumping. All the while there was a faint stirring in the dark corners of my mind, something clamoring for remembrance. Ah, yes! Standing on a dock long long years ago, looking down on a big oyster sloop, just docked after dumping a load of "seed". An old man in a derby hat working a pump just aft of the hatches—a square, wooden, built-in well from which there gushed a flood of foamy water, fanning across the deck and streaming through the scuppers in the rails.

It was probably the same kind of pump I had borrowed, and a type known to man for hundreds of years, but to me it was an exciting discovery. In the belief that there are others who take a curious interest in such simple things, I have felt justified in devoting this space to its story.

Last summer I met up with a second wooden bilge pump, a different type and rather unique. My good friend Robert Haight had invited me aboard his venerable Cape Cod catboat. He is inordinately proud of

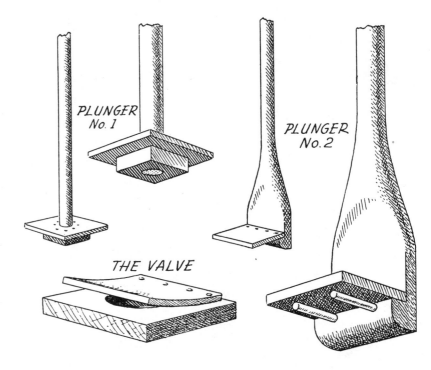

PLUNGER No. 1

PLUNGER No. 2

THE VALVE

the Edith, and well might he be, for it falls to the lot of very few boats to have the loving care of a sailor such as he. During the course of my visit he proudly pointed out that she had two built-in wooden bilge pumps, one on either side of her centerboard trunk, discharging onto the floor of her self bailing cockpit. The plunger is a very curious affair. A piece of oak, 1 by 3, has a shoulder cut in its lower end on which is tacked a pure gum rubber flapper ¼ inch thick. To prevent its collapsing on the up-stroke two bronze dowels or pins are fixed in the oak immediately beneath the rubber flapper, about as I have shown. The wood is reduced to a round section above to form a han-dle. A pretty neat affair, I say.

Upon sober reflection I will have to admit that wooden pumps are about as elementary and rude as man could devise, but like many other simple handmade tools of ancient origin they work beautifully. And as Bob Smith said, "They don't cost nothin' neither." What more could one ask?

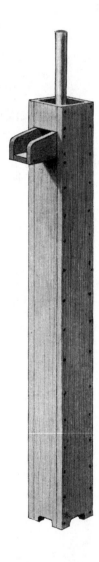

Palm and Needle Practice

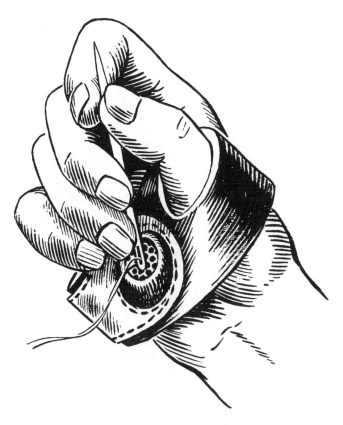

PROFICIENCY with the sail needle and sewing palm can only be attained by experience. I have noticed that few yachtsmen will take the time to practise on old scraps of canvas, but give a man a definite job such as a simple sail repair or the making of some practical item of ship's gear, and his interest is aroused. Here is an opportunity to get in some more sewing time and make something useful while doing it.

The bag shown here was originally made to carry ice, and it takes a fifty pound piece comfortably. However I soon discovered that it was also very handy for carrying groceries and duffel, so it really should be called a carry-all bag. It is entirely hand sewn.

The secret of sewing with a palm and needle lies

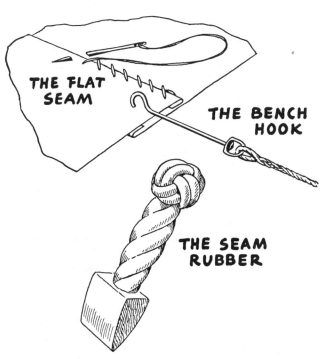

THE FLAT SEAM

THE BENCH HOOK

THE SEAM RUBBER

mainly in the way you hold the needle. Notice in the illustration that the needle is held near the point with the thumb and forefinger, and the eye of the needle is seated in the iron of the palm, held there by the middle finger. In use the hand is held flat to the canvas. Holding the needle as shown, it is started through the canvas, the point is regrasped by the thumb and forefinger as it emerges, and the eye is reseated in the iron by the middle finger the instant it clears the canvas. An experienced sailmaker does it in one quick smooth motion, rhythmically. In fact he hardly seems to let go of the needle at all. In contrast the amateur generally starts the needle with the fingers, then seats the eye in the iron, and tries to shove it through with outstretched hand! As a result the needle rarely goes where he wants it to go, it wobbles all over the place, and he harpoons his leg with every stitch.

Just remember that the needle should be held and seated in the palm at all times, except when actually passing through the canvas. You push with the whole arm, the wrist being more or less rigid.

The size of the needle is important—the heavier the cloth the larger the needle. In making this bag I used No. 6 canvas and a No. 13 needle. It is something you learn by experience.

Another point that amateurs do not seem to grasp is the necessity for using a bench hook. Watch a sailmaker, and you'll see that he sews with his work held flat on his lap, and it stays flat. Without a bench hook you draw the canvas all up in a bunch every time you take a stitch.

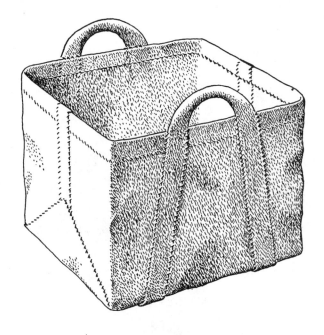

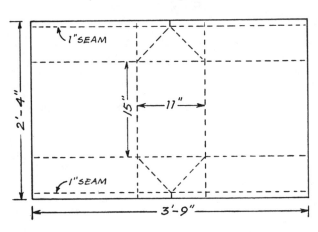

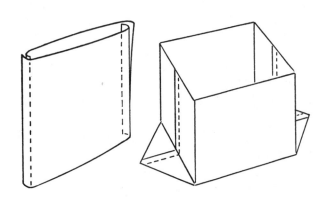

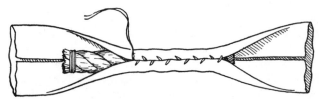

Since you always sew from right to left, the bench hook goes into the canvas somewhere near your right leg and is held by the lanyard, which is hitched securely to the nearest chair leg, or to your wife's if she is nearer.

A seam rubber, while not absolutely necessary, is a fine tool to have. You can't buy one, since they are always homemade. It is merely a wedge shaped tool of hard wood used to crease the canvas and smooth a seam. The one shown here is made of applewood, 3½ inches long, and the wedge is 1¼ inches wide.

So much for the tools. The flat seam I have shown is the one most commonly used. The length of the stitch is controlled by the angle at which the stitch crosses the seam. The spacing of the stitches is determined by the length of the needle, generally ten or twelve to the needle. Since I used a No. 13 needle, which is 3 inches long, I took twelve stitches in every 3 inches of seam.

To start the bag, lay out a piece of No. 6 canvas to the size shown in the diagram. The dashed lines, which represent seams and folds, should be drawn on the canvas with a soft pencil. Fold the canvas over from right to left. Now lap the edges 1 inch and pin together. Thread your needle with an arm's length of twine doubled, and wax it well. The beeswax strengthens the twine and prevents snarls. Twist the twine a bit by rolling it down your leg with the palm of your hand.

Lay an odd piece of canvas across your lap to prevent snagging your trousers. Now pick up the bag, hook in your bench hook and lash it fast. Remember that you sew with the edge of the seam away from you and work from right to left, the needle pointing towards you diagonally. Try to keep your stitches evenly spaced and aligned. Draw them up snugly, just enough to sink them in the canvas slightly. Be sure to turn the raw edges of the canvas under.

When both edges of the bag have been closed, turn it inside out and sew the other edges of the lapped seams. You will now have what looks like a canvas envelope. Open it up and fold it to the box-like shape shown in the third diagram. The triangle shaped ends are then turned up to meet the ends of the bag and sewed along their edges, as shown in the illustration of the finished bag.

Now turn the top edge of the bag down all around for an inch and a half seam. The seam, of course, should be on the inside of the bag. When this has been sewn you are ready for the handles.

Cut two pieces of canvas 4 feet 4 inches long by 4 inches wide. Fold the edges in until they meet, making two straps 2 inches wide. Now cut two pieces of ⅝ inch rope 6 inches long and whip the ends. Lay one of these in the center of one of the straps and sew it in as shown in the last illustration. Notice that the stitch used here is the baseball stitch.

When both straps are completed, sew them to the bag as shown, using the flat seam. The ends of the opposite straps should meet or overlap on the bottom of the bag.

THE DITTY-BAG
by
HERVEY GARRETT SMITH

COMPANION piece to the sea chest of olden days was the sailor's ditty bag. Hung from a hook by his bunk, it held his sewing gear and sundry articles necessary to the art of marlinespike seamanship. Here were his needles and palm, bench hook and pricker, sail twine and serving mallet, marlinespike and seam rubber. This last article is seldom seen nowadays, but every yachtsman should have one. Generally made of fruitwood or whalebone, it is a handy tool for creasing canvas and rubbing down a flat seam.

Ditty bags were from 6 to 8 inches in diameter and 12 to 15 inches deep, generally with a simple round bottom. Around the top were 4 to 8 holes, hand worked, into which the legs of the lanyard were spliced. The lanyards often were quite elaborate affairs, depending upon the skill and fancy of the sailor. Some had six or eight different kinds of sennit and as many different knots, the result being more fancy than practical.

The ditty bag shown here is one of the simpler types, fairly good looking and efficient, measuring 7½ by 12 inches with hexagonal bottom. Lay out your canvas accurately as shown in the diagram, marking the position of the holes, folds and seams in pencil. Cut it out and join the sides with a 1 inch flat seam, using doubled sail twine well waxed. Next close the six gores forming the bottom of the bag with a round seam. Fold the top down outside and flat-seam it all around, with the raw edge turned under. Now turn the bag right side out and you are ready for the worked holes.

Cut a 5/16 inch hole in the canvas and over it place a ⅜ inch grommet made from tarred yacht marline. This is sewn to the canvas all the way around, with the stitches completely hiding the grommet from view. When all six holes have been worked, your bag is finished and ready for the lanyard.

Take 3 pieces of ⅛ inch cotton line about 7 feet long and lay up a 3 strand braid or sennit in the middle. This braided section should be about 3 inches long. Bring the 2 ends of the braid together and clap on a seizing, forming

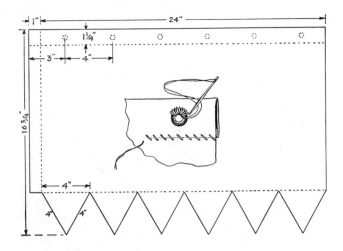

continue with a 6 strand round sennit, which is made by merely crowning the strands continuously to the right for a distance of 3 inches. Here you tie another Matthew Walker knot which completes the handle of the lanyard.

With a separate piece of cotton line make up a 3 strand Turk's head, shellac it and give it a coat of white paint. When dry, slip it over the 6 strands or legs of the lanyard. Sliding it up or down opens or closes the bag. Now splice the legs into the worked holes around the top of the bag. The total length of the lanyard from eye to bag should be 16 to 18 inches.

Stencil or stitch in colored wool your initials on the front of the bag and the job is done. Caution—don't ever hang your ditty bag on a thwartship bulkhead! A couple of days of sailing and you will find the bag worn through and the bulkhead neatly grooved.

an eye with 6 long strands depending from it. With these strands tie a 6 strand double Matthew Walker knot. Now

THE
HITCHED EYELET

The Sea Bag

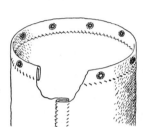

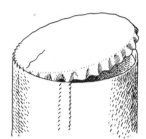

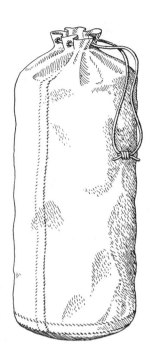

TO YACHTSMEN who need some palm and needle practice, which means about nine out of ten, the making of a hand sewn sea bag offers an excellent opportunity to acquire greater skill, and a useful piece of gear. Few indeed can match the expertness of the professional sailmaker at hand sewing, and constant practice is still the only means of achieving perfection. It is for that purpose alone that this article is presented.

Sea bags are so familiar to all that it is hardly necessary to go into a discourse on their history and use. Generally speaking, we associate them with the Navy, both of the present and the past, and their use is probably as ancient as the sea chest of the merchantman. Yachtsmen like them because they are easy to stow, since they can be crammed into almost any shape of compartment, and they do not rattle!

The nicest thing about making your own bag is that the size can be tailored to your needs. Most bags seem to be about 1 foot in diameter by 3 deep, the wider the mouth the shorter the bag as a rule. In my opinion 14 inches by slightly less than 3 feet is a convenient size, as too small a diameter makes it difficult to fish out an article which happens to be at the bottom of the bag. Nine ounce duck or heavier should be used, and of course the heavier weights are harder to sew.

Cut a piece of canvas 36 by 47 inches for the sides, which will make a bag 14 by 32½ inches. The cutaway drawing at the top of this page shows how the bag is formed with a flat seam and the method of lapping the two edges of the cloth. First I suggest you lay out the folds with pencil guide lines. Draw a line parallel to and 1½ inches from each 36 inch edge, as guides for folding

the sides. Across the top draw a line 1½ inches down, and another one 1½ inches below that. These are guides for the double fold around the top of the bag. Across the bottom draw a line one-half inch from the edge, which is a guide for sewing in the bottom.

Fold the 36 inch edges over and crease the folds with a seam rubber, or any smooth object. Now "hook" the two folds together and sew a flat seam, about 4 stitches to the inch, with well waxed doubled sail twine. Turn the bag inside out and sew the other edge. The tubular body of the bag is now formed, and the top comes next. Turn the top edge down upon itself twice, on the 2 pencil guide lines, and stitch the edge down. Now turn the bag inside out, which places the turned-down flap inside the bag, as shown in the first sketch.

Six or eight eyelets must be worked around the top of the bag to take the lanyard or drawstring. "Boughten" sea bags come equipped with wrought brass grommets set in with a die, and they are perfectly satisfactory, but the marlinspike sailor of the old school would insist on hand worked eyelets. They take longer to make, but after all we want needle practice, so we will do it the hard way and get a handsomer job. Locate the eyelets evenly about the top with a pencil mark. Punch a hole through the three thicknesses of canvas with an awl, and over the hole place a one-half inch grommet of marline. Now thread two lengths of sail twine in your needle and wax them well, then stitch the grommet down evenly until it is completely hidden. The peculiar type of stitch used results in a series of hitches round about, hence it is called a "hitched eyelet", and the sketch shows how it is made. Most amateurs do poorly when it comes to making eyelets, and I think it is because they can't visualize perfectly aligned stitches. Therefore I suggest that you draw a penciled circle with a compass as a guide for entering the needle in the canvas. Keep your stitches evenly spaced and with equal tension throughout.

For the bottom of the bag you will need a circular piece of canvas 16 inches in diameter. Draw a penciled circle 1 inch from the edge, or 14 inches diameter, as a guide for stitches. Fold or crease the canvas on this line and insert the bottom in the up-ended bag, as shown in the second illustration. Now stitch the edge of the bag to the penciled line of the bottom. Next turn the bag inside out, fold the 1 inch flap of the bottom piece down over the sides of the bag and stitch it fast. The third illustration shows this step completed, and you will note that the canvas flap of the bottom has to be crimped or gathered as you stitch, to take up the excess material.

Now turn the bag right side out and reeve a lanyard through the eyelets. Braided cotton line about 3/16 inch diameter and 48 inches long is about right for this, and the ends are joined with a double overhand bend.

The Bell Rope

BACK in the heyday of the American clipper the shipboard visitor could hardly fail to notice the efficient looking ship's bell, in fact two of them—the small one near the big steering wheel on which the helmsman struck the half hours, and the really big one on the forecastle abaft the windlass by which the lookout answered him.

So also today even the smallest auxiliary carries a ship's bell as required by law, but the average yachtsman generally tosses it into a locker where it lies forgotten until the day arrives when he suddenly needs it, whereupon he discovers it has no bell rope.

Now your old time sailor, to whom the making of so common a thing as a bell rope was a labor of love rather than a chore, would have welcomed the opportunity to display his talents and would have proceeded straightforth with infinite care and patience, as though his life depended on it. The result would be a bell rope useful and handsome, and many years and many ships later it would still be doing its duty, a monument to a simple sailor who knew his craft and took pride in the knowing.

So drag that old bell out from under the after deck where it has lain since 1927, polish it up until it glitters, and fit it out with a real old time bell rope, sailor fashion.

[87]

I'll warrant you will not hide it again, but will keep it handy where friends can see and admire it. Which is as it should be!

The bell rope shown here is a rather simple example and easy to make. It took me about four hours. Four 12 foot lengths of white cotton rope were middled and a 2½ inch section laid up into a 4 strand flat sennit braid. This was doubled to form an eye or becket and a seizing clapped on. Then the 8 strands were divided into pairs and a square sennit worked a distance of 3 inches by alternately crowning the 4 pairs of strands first to the right and then to the left. Here the 8 strands were seized and all the slack worked out of the sennit by pulling up each bight in turn with a crochet hook.

The handle required a solid core, for which I used a 4 inch piece of wooden dowel. The 8 strands were continuously crowned to the right around this core and a seizing put on the end. The pattern formed by the crowning had a tendency to spiral to the right somewhat, so it was necessary to twist the whole works to the left in order to get the bights aligned vertically. The slack was taken out carefully until all the strands were tight and the core completely hidden.

To finish off the end, the strands were again paired and made up into a double wall and crown knot. Around the base of this knot was placed a 4 strand Turk's head. A 3 strand Turk's head next to the eye or becket, and a 2 strand Turk's head in the middle completed the job. The finished bell rope was then shellacked and given two coats of semigloss white paint. This treatment fills up the interstices between the strands and gives a weatherproof finish.

The becket was secured to the striker or clapper of the bell by a lashing of marline.

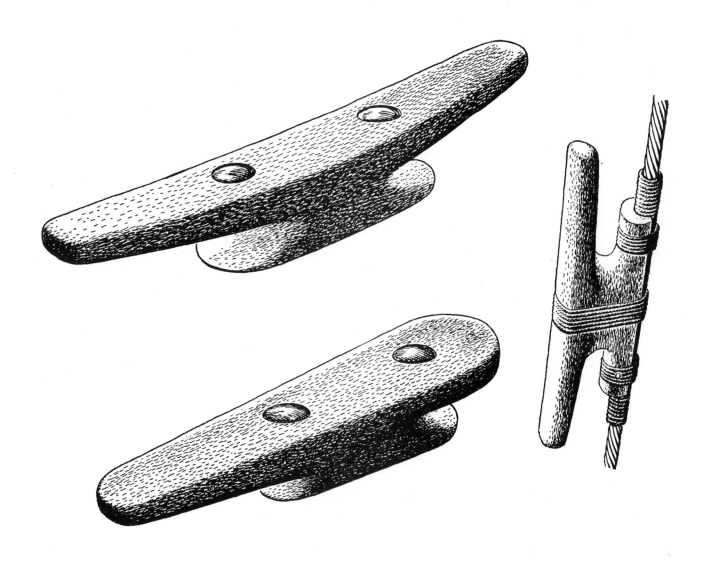

Wooden Cleats

TO THE yachtsman who likes to make his own fittings, nothing gives more satisfaction than wooden cleats. When properly designed, they are easier on rope than their metal counterparts. Having more surface area, resting in more friction, the rope is less liable to slip. They have a rugged honest appearance that appeals to all sailors.

The cleats shown here are ones that I have made and used for many years, and while I do not claim they are perfect, they have always proven satisfactory. In fact I would not go to sea without them. They are made of locust, well seasoned and close grained, and were soaked in hot linseed oil when finished.

The first is an all purpose cleat designed to handle ⅜ or ½ inch rope. The blank was roughed out on the bandsaw to the dimensions given. The horns were rounded off with a wood rasp, and the neck or throat was hollowed with a rat-tail file. Sandpaper removed all the high spots and gave it the final shape. It was bored to take two ¼ inch carriage bolts, the heads being slightly countersunk.

The second cleat shown is a jam cleat for ⅜ inch

rope, and was designed to handle jibsheets on a small centerboarder where speed in handling was of prime importance. The sheet can be led around the wide after end and held in the hand, the cleat thus acting as a deck block or fairleader. To belay, the hauling part is pulled across under the long horn where it is jammed securely between the horn and the deck. To release, give it a jerk and it is free to run. It is secured to the deck by carriage bolts.

The last item is a shroud cleat to belay flag halliards. In days gone by it would probably have been made of whalebone, but lignum vitae, if obtainable, is the best substitute. It was designed for 3/16 inch wire rigging, which is parceled with friction tape and served with marline for a length of 4 inches, to which the cleat is seized. After the blank is roughed out it is finished with a file, shallow grooves are cut to receive the seizings, and the base is hollowed out with a rat-tail file to fit the served shroud. The cleat is mounted breast high on the *after side* of the shroud and secured by three seizings of tarred yacht marline, drawn up as tightly as possible and then given three coats of spar varnish.

Regardless of whether you varnish or paint them, wooden cleats should first be soaked a long time in hot linseed oil until the wood is saturated. This prevents any tendency to check, and seems to harden the wood considerably. Allow at least three days for the oil to harden before varnishing.

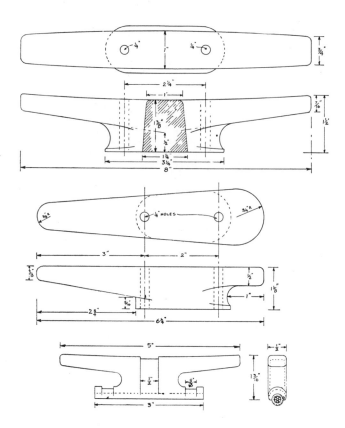

Rope Fenders

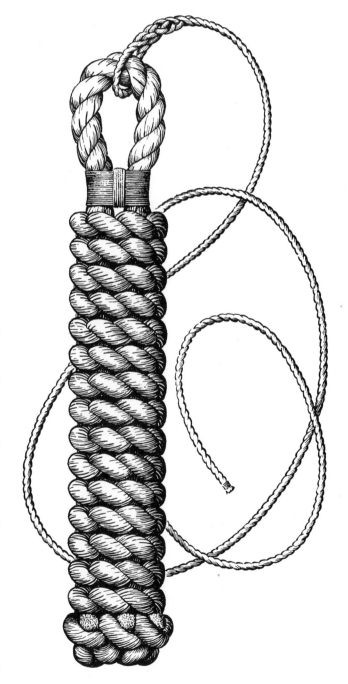

IF I were to evaluate the thousands of applications of the art of marlinespike seamanship I would place the sea chest becket at the top of the list, and way down at the bottom would be the lowly rope fender. The chest becket deserves the honor because it is the highest form of the sailor's art, but all we ask of a fender is that it suffer violent shocks and protect a boat's hull from damage. Beauty is something not generally associated with fenders. Canvas wrapped auto tires do not rank as works of art no matter how practical they may be.

But in spite of its lowly origin, made as it is of salvaged material, I can still see beauty in a well made rope fender. That is the amazing thing about rope—its inherent, dormant, potential beauty. The minute you unlay a piece of rope and rearrange the strands it begins to acquire character and design, the degree of art attained being limited only by your skill and ingenuity.

The simple fender shown here requires only an elementary knowledge of rope work and very little skill to make. On second thought I suppose I should qualify that statement before someone makes an issue of the degree of skill required. To be candid, shortly after you start the fender you imagine yourself wrestling with an ambidextrous octopus, and before you are finished you sort of wish you were an octopus.

Middle a 20 foot length of ¾ or 1 inch rope and form an eye with a stout seizing of marline as shown. Unlay the strands of both parts to the seizing. Now hold the eye between your knees and form a wall knot with the six strands. On top of this form two or three more walls. Do not draw the strands up tight, but just enough for the wall to hold its shape. Cut a 12 inch length of common garden hose and insert it in the walls you have formed. This acts as a waterproof core for the fender, gives it resilience and keeps it from losing its shape. With the hose in place, continue walling the strands until you reach the top.

Now go back to the first wall and with your marlinespike proceed to draw up the strands tightly. Do not try to follow one strand the full length of the fender, but rather tighten each wall in turn. When the last wall is reached you will find the strands have snugged down, leaving some of the hose protruding. Add more walls and tighten up until the hose is completely hidden.

To finish off the fender crown the strands over the end of the hose, tuck the ends through the last wall and cut them off. Splice a 5 or 6 foot length of ¼ inch cotton rope to the eye of the fender and it is ready for use.

Most fenders of this type have a core composed of rope which has been unlaid, chopped up and crammed in. This soaks up water and never dries out, therefore I use rubber hose. Another variation is to crown the strands instead of walling them. But whether you wall or crown,

the result is a good looking practical fender that will last for years and cost you nothing.

For three years now the Morning Star has been moored at a bulkhead, her topsides protected by what was once a good anchor cable, but converted on a rainy Sunday afternoon to rope fenders such as these. They squeak as she surges slowly back and forth on her spring lines, and a mighty comforting sound it is, for I know they are doing their job. By the time they are worn out I'll have accumulated the makings for some new ones— old rope that is "too poor to use and too good to throw away."

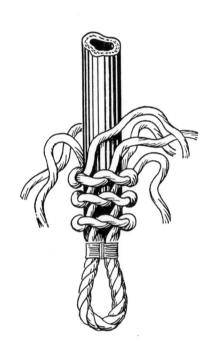

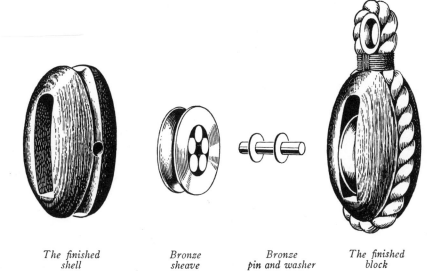

The finished shell   *Bronze sheave*   *Bronze pin and washer*   *The finished block*

Stropped Blocks

HAVE you ever tossed in your bunk on a windy night, cussing the noisy deck block clattering and banging away just above your ear?

Do your jibsheet blocks wham into the foreside of your mast every time you go about, leaving unsightly gouges and scars?

Have you ever secretly yearned for some of the picturesque gear of the old squareriggers, deadeyes and lanyards, tarred hemp and canvas buckets, salt horse casks and handy billies?

If so, you need some rope stropped blocks. Time was when all blocks were rope stropped. They were made in endless variety, each designed for a specific job, tested and proved through years of hard usage. Handmade by men who took pride in their craft, they had a salty authentic look, and they still have that look.

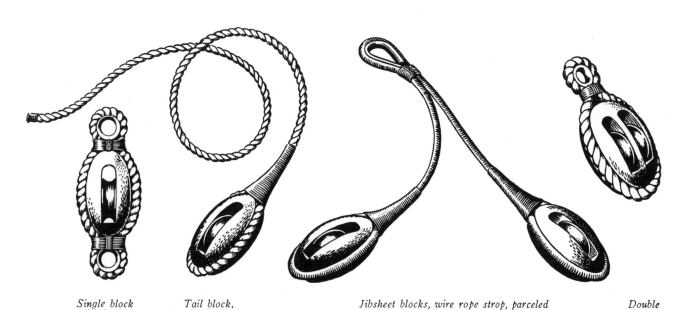

Single block with becket   *Tail block, spliced strop*   *Jibsheet blocks, wire rope strop, parceled and served*   *Double block*

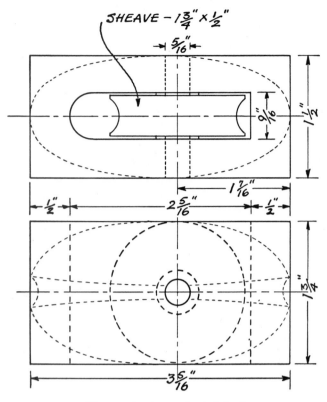

SHEAVE – 1¾" x ½"

Diagram showing mechanical details

thread, the same rope your sailmaker uses for roping sails. Some brass manila rope thimbles and a ball of tarred Italian hemp marline will complete your list of materials needed.

First, get out the shell blank to the dimensions shown, being sure it is square all around. Lay out the construction lines accurately with a scriber or sharp awl. Now bore the pinhole, preferably with a drill press as it is imperative that the hole be exactly at right angles to the mortise.

Next, bore for the mortise and clean out with a chisel. Use a file or rasp in finishing and be sure the sides are true and smooth.

Taper the blank to the shape shown in dotted lines with a chisel and then start rounding off with a rasp. When reasonably true and smooth, cut in the strop grooves with a rat-tail file. Clean up with fine sandpaper and the shell is ready for finishing.

While the shell may be varnished an oil finish is preferable, as the wood pores are more completely filled and checking is prevented. Submerge the shell in a can of raw linseed oil and heat until it starts to boil. Cook it for one-half hour or three hours. The longer you cook it, the better it will be. Then wipe the shell dry and set aside for a week or so to harden. You will get a durable weatherproof finish which will not mar or check.

To assemble, pack the sheave bushing with water pump grease, place a washer on each side, slip it into the mortise and press in the pin. The pin should fit the shell rather tightly, and the ends should be flush, not riveted.

The strop is merely a hemp grommet, and the size can only be determined by trial and error. If you have never made a grommet you can learn how very easily by referring to any good book on rope work and splicing. When placed on the block, with the thimble in position, the grommet should fit snugly.

Clap on a throat seizing as shown, drawing it up as tightly as possible with a Spanish windlass. Finish off with a couple of cross turns and a square knot. Your block is now finished.

After a couple of season's use cut off the strop, force out the pin, repack the sheave with grease and reassemble. Put on a new grommet and seizing and your block is as good as new.

This is a basic design and you can take it from there. Many variations can be worked out easily for specific uses. For a double block merely increase the dimensions of the blank shown to accommodate another mortise, with a ½ inch separator.

But aside from their romantic appeal to the sailor's eye they have certain inherent advantages not possessed by their modern counterparts. Above all, a rope stropped block is quiet. There are no exposed metal parts; the strop is a built-in fender. It cushions the shock of impact and saves wear and tear on spars and gear. Furthermore, if made properly it is perfectly streamlined from all angles and hence is positively nonfouling.

Inexpensive and easy to make, these blocks will give character to your little Annie B as nothing else can. Try them and notice the change that comes over Annie,

While the block shown here is for ⅜ inch rope, you can change the dimensions proportionately for other sizes. The sheaves can be had from most ship chandlers or marine supply houses. Be sure they are roller bushed. A length of bronze rod will furnish the pins, with some brass washers to fit.

For the shells you will need some well seasoned, tough, close grained wood. Locust is ideal, and your best source of supply will probably be an old fence post. It will be hard as a rock and difficult to work, so be sure your tools are sharp. The strops should be of tarred hemp, twelve

Canvas Deck Bucket

ONE of the most useful and seldom found articles aboard a boat today is a good deck bucket. Note that we say good. To many boat owners that means a common galvanized iron pail, but an iron pail is neither a deck bucket nor good. It is just a danged old noisy piece of hardware that bangs up your brightwork and cannot be stowed in the right place.

Back in the days when there were more sailors than hardware salesmen, ships' buckets were either canvas or cedar. The cedar buckets were generally made ashore by a cooper, but the canvas ones were more often made on board ship by a sailor, with the materials at hand and time enough to do a good job.

In these days of small craft and limited stowage space a deck bucket should be a canvas one. You can buy one,

to be sure, but it will probably be a flimsy affair which will collapse like a tired sock when set down on deck. Make your own, sailor fashion, and add another piece of gear you can be proud of.

You will need a piece of number four canvas about 15 by 33 inches. Don't make the mistake of asking for "four ounce". Heavy canvas goes by number, not weight. This will make a bucket 9 inches in diameter by about 11 inches deep. You also will need a 9 inch wooden mast hoop for the rim, and a 9 inch disk of ⅜ inch waterproof plywood for the bottom. This last item is where we abandon tradition and go modern.

The first step is to sew up your canvas with a doubled seam, as shown in the illustration, to form a cylinder or tube exactly 9 inches in diameter. Use your plywood disk as a guide for measuring. With your needle and palm and a doubled length of well waxed sail twine, sew up one edge of the seam, turn inside out and finish off the other edge.

Now take an odd piece of ½ inch or ⅝ inch rope and make up a rope grommet with an outside diameter of exactly 9 inches Place this inside the canvas tube at one end, turn the raw edge of the canvas under, and sew it fast, just as the boltrope is sewn to your sail. This serves as a fender on the bottom of the bucket, as well as a hand hold when emptying it.

With a rat-tail file cut a groove in the edge of the plywood disk about one-eighth inch deep. Sand it smooth, give it three coats of paint, and when dry push it down inside the canvas until it rests on the rope grommet. Secure it by taking several turns around the outside with a length of serving wire. Draw it up tightly so the canvas is forced into the groove in the plywood, twist the ends and fasten with a copper tack.

Next place your mast hoop around the top and turn the canvas down over it about 2 inches. Turn the raw edge under and sew neatly all around. In this seam just under the hoop make two worked eyelets opposite each other to take the bail. To make a worked eyelet, punch or cut a ⅜ inch hole through the canvas and over it place a miniature grommet, ½ inch in diameter, made out of tarred marline. Proceed to sew this in place, making a complete turn of close stitches around the eyelet.

Splice a ⅜ inch rope bail or becket into the eyelets, and secure a brass thimble in the bight of it with a round seizing of marline. Into the seized eye thus formed splice a ½ inch rope pennant, and finish off the end with a manrope knot, or any fancy end knot that appeals to you.

There, sailor, is a real deck bucket. It will stow like an opera hat, stand up when it is supposed to and, with your boat's name neatly painted on, it will look as though it belonged on board.

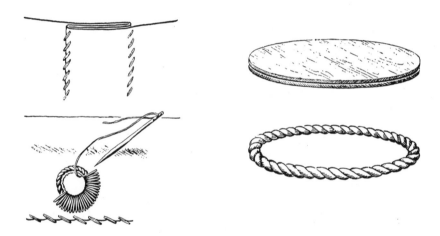

Rigging a Jackline

IN THE interest of fair play, let it be known that I have never rigged a jackline in my life nor have I ever sailed in a yacht equipped with one. I disclaim all responsibility for this chapter in its entirety since it was literally forced upon me, the culmination of long years of ignorance and suffering.

Looking back in retrospect, my entire life has been bedeviled by jib trouble. In fact I don't recollect ever owning a jib that really behaved itself or showed any regard for my feelings in the slightest. Fate apparently intended that I should be a catboat sailor and I was too headstrong to admit it. But while there's life there's hope, and as long as I am able to let out a seam and plane down a batten I intend to pursue the unattainable—the perfect jib.

The first jib of which I have any recollection was an ancient affair I "found", draped carelessly over several barrels of deceased fish. Using this as bait, I had no trouble at all in convincing my best friend that his cat rigged rowboat would be vastly improved if rigged as a sloop. On her trial trip in the teeth of a gentle southerly she turned end for end and sank slowly out of sight, ballasted as she was with the flywheel from an old Standard gas engine. This then should have been an omen, a warning to lay off jibs and stick to catboats, but being young and foolish I ignored it, and now, many jibs and many boats later, here I sit toying with the idea of a newfangled jib rigged with a jackline.

In my boyhood most of the sloops in my home waters were rigged with sprit jibs, a practice which was undoubtedly a fad and soon was discarded. The sprit caused the jib to set abominably on one tack since it cut into the sail on the lee side and disturbed the normal flow of the wind over the surface. The only point in its favor was that it permitted the use of a single part, self trimming sheet.

For the better part of my life I have sailed with the common garden variety of jibs, the loose footed type. This kind is so universally used and

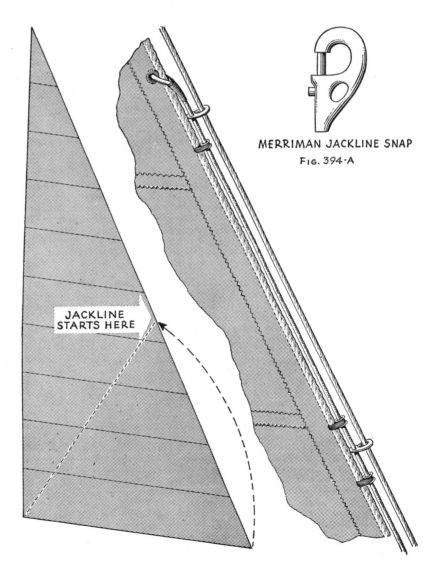

MERRIMAN JACKLINE SNAP
FIG. 394-A

JACKLINE
STARTS HERE

so well known that comment seems hardly necessary. Everyone knows that a loose footed jib, properly cut and properly set, gives an almost perfect airfoil and a high degree of efficiency. For a racing boat it is a must. Indeed it is often considered to be more important in windward work than the mainsail, in terms of efficiency. But somehow I never was able to achieve that ideal. The perfect jib was somehow always on that other boat to windward of me, pointing high and footing like the proverbial bat out of.

With me it was always a case of fluttering leech, sagging luff, broken battens and backwinded mainsail. My deck was a sieve of plugged up holes from shifted deck leads. My beloved eighteen footer after fifteen years of racing had the largest complement of recut, reroped, repaired and altered jibs ever seen in these parts. Even today, some five years after she was sold, come spring housecleaning time I am as liable as not to come across another jib or two. But under her new owner, ironically enough, her jibs work like a charm and give no trouble whatsoever!

For all its efficiency a loose footed jib has one undesirable feature. It requires double sheets which must be handled each time you go about. Now with a well trained crew this is no problem at all, but when you sail single handed it is another story.

Tacking down a narrow stream alone, with mainsheet, tiller, backstays and jibsheets to tend every ten seconds, sort of wears you down and you begin to think of catboats again. But hope springs eternal, so I sat down to design my dream boat, the one in which all previous problems would be solved, and the jib could take care of itself.

Then came the memorable day when the ketch Morning Star got under way on her trial trip under sail. Never will I forget the palpitating heart, the humble thanksgiving for all the long suppressed desires coming into fruition. Ah, this is the life! Look at that jib up there, setting pretty as a picture. She has a nine foot club with a single sheet. Want to put her about? Just put her helm down and she'll come around without touching a sheet. Yes sir, the self tending, club footed jib is well nigh perfect. Or is it?

Starting up the motor, we headed into the wind and I went forward to douse the sails. As I bent over to cast off the jib halliard that "efficient" jib club whammed across the deck, catching me right between the doghouse and the fence, and I almost swallowed my pivot tooth. As soon as I recovered my dignity I lowered away smartly, and the club slid forward and jammed between the bowsprit and the bowsprit shrouds. I commenced to get an old familiar feeling. Stopping it neatly to its club, I struggled manfully to get that jib below and up in the forepeak. It snagged all six starboard shrouds on the way aft, nearly brained my crew, and down below there's a gouge in the forward bulkhead I have never succeeded in hiding.

When I was sure I was alone I sat down on a bunk and cried quietly into my brand new deck-bucket. Through the port I saw two happy carefree kids sailing serenely up the creek in a little catboat. No jibsheets. No jib club. No jib.

Several years have passed since that day and I have reached the end of my rope, and my jibs. A compassionate friend has advised me that rigging a jackline on my jib and installing a full length jib boom will put an end to all my troubles. According to him, it has worked successfully on his yacht, is self trimming, and keeps the sail under better control when lowering away. Of course it can still knock you overboard if you get careless, but at least the boom is secured at one end, and the sail is easily stripped off for stowing in a sailbag.

After examining my friend's jib and observing its performance I made the accompanying illustrations. With a full length jib boom it is impossible to lower the jib on the stay completely without the use of a jackline, which is fairly obvious. Spreading your jib out flat, you swing an arc up from the tack, with the clew as a center. Where the arc intersects the luff is the point at which the jackline is attached. A light, well stretched line is spliced into a worked grommet at this point and runs alternately through snap hooks on the stay and small brass thimbles which are seized to the jib roping. The two thimbles at each snaphook are about three inches apart. The Merriman snaphook which I have shown is made expressly for this purpose. When the jib is fully hoisted the jackline is pulled taut and secured to the tack cringle. When furled, the jackline's being free to slide through the thimbles enables the lower part of the luff to pull away from the stay. Of course the foot of the jib has slides and runs on sail track on the boom, and the orthodox clew outhaul fitting is used. However I have been advised that providing your jib is miter cut you can also set it loose footed, giving you just that much more latitude in its use. A fixed boom also permits the employment of a wide variety of sheet leads, a desirable feature.

So there, I hope, is the answer to my problem of how to achieve a controllable foolproof jib. It will probably result in a complete set of new problems, but I can't help feeling it will be a success. It has to, for I have tried everything else.

Sail Stop Bag

BACK in the days when we owned a small sloop, sail stops were of minor importance. Just a few were needed and they were always within reach. But upon graduating to a thirty-three foot ketch they became a major problem. Not only were there a lot more of them, but they were always in the wrong place. In fact they were all over the ship.

Reach into a locker for a fender and come up with a sail stop. Grab a dock line off the pin rail and sail stops would be fouled in the coil. Cast off the mizzen halliard and watch a sail stop go aloft with it. But try to muzzle the mainsail single handed in a stiff breeze, and all but one would be down below in the forward berth behind the pillow! Hence this sail stop bag.

Take an eight inch wooden mast hoop, sanded and varnished, and clove hitch a row of loops around it with a small white cotton fish line, using a seine or netting needle. When the row is completed tie the ends together. Now start a second row of loops or meshes, using the mesh knot shown in the diagram, and continue until the cylindrical net is about twelve or fourteen inches deep. To close the bag, reeve a heavy cord through the last row of loops, draw it up tightly and tie securely.

This makes a stop bag that is hard to beat. The mouth is always open and rigid. If the stops are wet, they will dry quickly since air can circulate through them easily. Because of the mast hoop it can be hung on a belaying pen either empty or full, and if it goes over the side it will float.

But best of all, it keeps your sail stops right where they belong—all in one place.

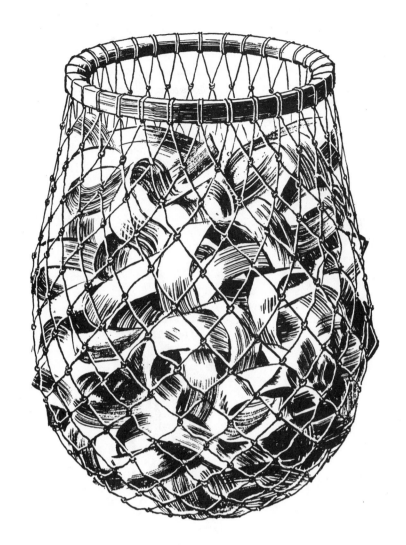

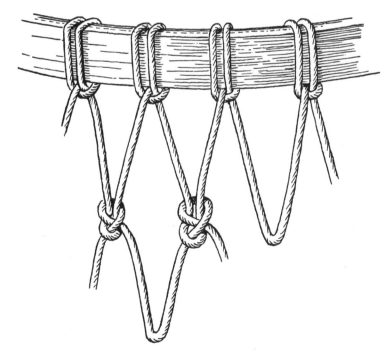

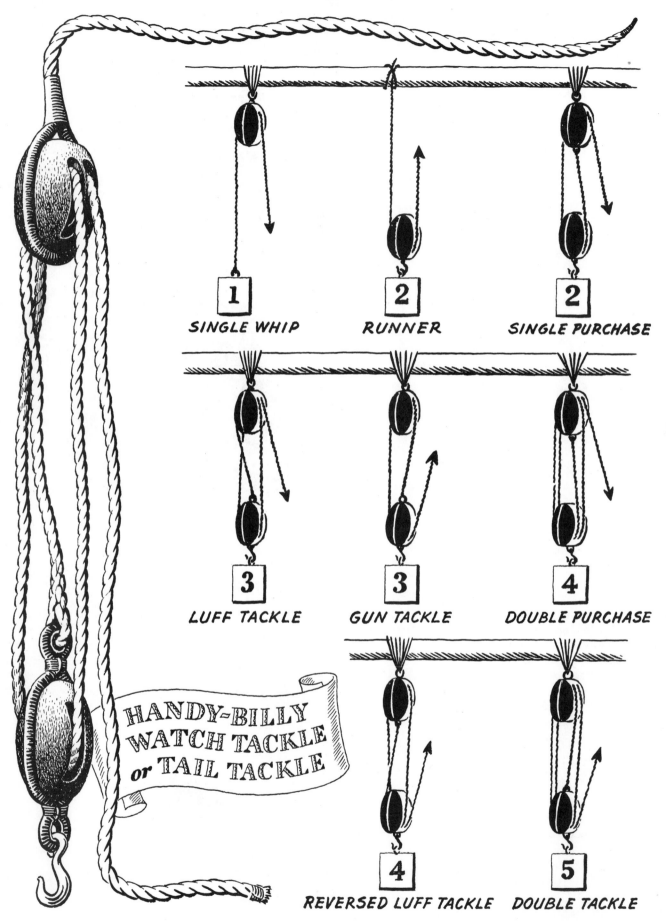

SINGLE WHIP

RUNNER

SINGLE PURCHASE

LUFF TACKLE

GUN TACKLE

DOUBLE PURCHASE

HANDY-BILLY
WATCH TACKLE
or TAIL TACKLE

REVERSED LUFF TACKLE

DOUBLE TACKLE

Some Notes on the Use of "Taykles"

JUST why the sailor pronounces the word "tackle" in the above manner, and contrary to the authority of the best English dictionaries, is a mystery. But "taykle" it is and always has been, and in the language of the sea the sailor's usage is authority enough.

The notes here set forth are elementary, serving merely as an introduction for the amateur yachtsman, for the beginner who is anxious to learn the fundamentals. Tackles are in some instances rather involved mechanisms, and to one who desires to dig into the subject at greater length I suggest an authoritative book such as Knight's *Modern Seamanship,* which is quite complete.

Definitely a tackle consists of a rope called the *fall* and one or more blocks through which it is *rove.* The purpose of a tackle is generally to gain an increase in power, and in some instances merely to change the direction in which the power is applied. An increase in the number of sheaves in the blocks over which the fall passes results in an increase in power up to a certain point, beyond which friction becomes such an enormous factor that it nullifies all theoretical power gained by the multiplicity of parts. Friction can use up anywhere from ten to seventy-five per cent of the force applied. To that must be added the weight of the tackle itself, which is why a complicated arrangement is of doubtful value.

The blocks in a tackle are either fixed or movable. Many yachtsmen have difficulty remembering how to determine the power gained with any given tackle. Just count the number of parts of rope entering the movable block and you have the answer. For example, if there are four it means that a pull of 100 pounds would move a 400 pound weight, with no allowance for friction.

On the opposite page I have shown eight simplified diagrams of the more common tackles, and the numeral in each weight represents the power or advantage gained in theory, no allowance for friction being made.

The first is the single whip, which represents no increase in power, the pull and the lift being equal. The fixed block merely changes the direction of pull. The simple one part halliard on a small boat is a typical application, the fixed block being the masthead sheave and the weight being the mainsail.

The runner is a single whip reversed. The block is movable, and since two parts of rope are entering it an advantage of two is gained. A pull of 100 pounds upward on the hauling part will lift 200 pounds.

The single purchase has two single blocks, with the fall leading from the fixed block. The movable block is called the fall block. Like the runner, the power of two is gained. It should be noted that any tackle in which both blocks have the same number of sheaves is properly called a purchase.

The luff tackle gives the power of three, and consists of a fixed double block and a movable single block. We'll have more to say about this later on.

The gun tackle also has the power of three, and is a single purchase reversed, having two single blocks. As its name denotes, it was the tackle used to haul guns through the ports in the days of the old muzzle loaders.

The double purchase has two double blocks and gives the power of four.

The reversed luff tackle has a fixed single block and a double fall block, giving the power of four.

The double tackle, consisting of two double blocks with the fall leading to the movable block gives the power of five.

These are the simple tackles, the ones most commonly used for a multitude of jobs. There are many others, each for a specific purpose and all necessary to the yachtsman who goes to sea in sail. A comprehensive knowledge of tackles is an important part of marlinspike seamanship all too often neglected, and that is the reason I urge you to pursue the subject to the saturation point.

Framing the diagrams on the opposite page is a handy billy, a tackle which should be in the rope locker of every yacht carrying sails. It is a small luff tackle with a short rope tail on the double block and a hook on the single block. It has more uses than any tackle I know, and with a power of three (four if reversed) it makes any hauling job easier. This is the tackle you use with your bosun's chair. Used as a jig on a jibsheet it is a poor man's winch. Bent to a broken shroud and hooked to a chainplate it is a turnbuckle to get you home without losing your mast. As a reefing tackle it is perfect.

The rope tail is about two or three feet long, with the end tapered to a point for ease in passing through a shackle or thimble. You will notice that I show rope strapped blocks, which is just a bit of propaganda creeping in. So firmly convinced am I of the superiority of rope strapped blocks over the "boughten" kind that I would stoop to almost any trick in order to bring light to the heathen.

A Lanyard for a Cannon

FROM a Rhode Island lady of seafaring ancestry I received a most interesting letter, from which, with her permission, I quote in part: "Today, being the day before the Fourth, I went hunting up in the top of the barn among the relics of the dear old roaring 'twenties. Among the brass ship's lanterns, binnacles, code flags, et cetera, I found what I was looking for, the little old saluting cannon, which I dragged out and oiled up, to put aboard the dinky little lobsterman for the morrow. But though I knotted up a lanyard for it as best my talents would permit, it looks like a dog leash, or something."

"Would you," she asked, "tell me how to produce a good salty looking item for my little old .12 gauge? There must be a whale of a lot of saluting cannons on yacht club porches from here to the Pacific that could do with a good looking lanyard instead of the bedraggled old knotted ropes they now sport."

"Anything to oblige a lady," said I, and shoved off for the races, the yacht Morning Star having been commandeered by the local club to serve as committee boat. The race committee being short handed as usual, I was pressed into service as gunner's mate, and upon being introduced to my weapon discovered what the Rhode Island lady had already surmised—that it sported a "bedraggled old knotted rope" in lieu of a proper lanyard.

So here is a gun lanyard I hope will please my correspondent and cause yacht clubs from coast to coast to look to their cannon. It is not very difficult to construct, nor is it very ornate, and should the maker's skill be limited it can be simplified to suit. All that is required in the making of lanyards is a working familiarity with a few simple sennits and decorative lanyard knots.

A proper gun lanyard should be about 30 inches long, and should be made of cotton line not over 3/32 inch in diameter. Untarred cod line or seine twine will do, but braided cotton is better. Take 6 strands about 50 inches long and bind them together with a stout seizing 6 inches from one end. These 6 inch ends will be used later to tie the end knot of the "handle". The handle section is 6 strand alternate crown sennit, and is the first section to be worked. Each succeeding section has one less strand, thus giving a nice taper to the lanyard. Because of space limitations the illustration is not to scale.

Elsewhere in this book I described the making of crown sennits. You will find it difficult to work with 50 inch strands, as they will constantly become entangled. To get around this merely wrap each strand around the fingers of one hand to form a small skein or coil and slip a rubber band around it. 6 inches will be enough sennit for the handle, and when completed put a seizing on to prevent it from loosening.

Now go back to the point of beginning, and with the free ends work a double diamond knot as shown. Note that the strands emerge from the top of the knot, where they are then cut off. The diamond knot, either single or doubled, is an excellent lanyard knot to know, and is capable of many variations. To work it, hold in the left hand below the seizing with the strands turned back all around. Take any strand and pass it to the right over and outside of the adjacent strand, and up under the second strand as shown. Now take the next strand to the right and pass to the right in a like manner, and continue until all 6 strands have been passed. To double the knot, each strand is passed again to the right, following below the adjacent strand until it emerges at the top of the knot once more. Draw

THE SINGLE DIAMOND KNOT

each strand up snugly until the knot is firm and hides the seizing, and then cut off the strands.

The second knot, which finishes off the alternate crown sennit, is a 6 strand Matthew Walker knot, the making of which was described on page 39. When completed and drawn up firmly (it requires some arranging of the strands to make them lie uniformly) cut off one of the strands where it emerges, thus leaving 5 strands with which a 6 inch section of continuous right

crown sennit is next worked. This gives an effect similar to cable laid rope. It is finished off with a 5 strand single diamond knot.

Now cut off one strand, and with the remaining 4 lay up 6 inches of plaited sennit, which is described elsewhere. Finish it off with a doubled wall knot and continue with a short section of four strand alternate crown sennit. Next tie a 4 strand single diamond and cut off one strand.

With the 3 remaining strands lay up a section of 3 strand rope, *right laid* if you are using braided line, *left laid* if cod line. Put on a seizing, lay out one strand, and twist the other 2 strands up into a cord or rope. Double it back on itself to form a loop and secure with a stout seizing. Then with the strand which was laid out tie a 2 strand running Turk's head about the body, hiding the seizing. Seize the loop to the trigger of your cannon, and you are all set for a fight or a frolic.

The Catboat Race

GRANDFATHER certainly had a nice privy. At least that was the sober opinion of a small boy some forty-odd years ago.

Facing east to receive the warming rays of the morning sun, as a proper privy should, it stood just to starboard of the workshop, discreetly shielded from the curious eye by a lattice drenched with honeysuckle. In a day when life was a little more rugged, its seats were neatly covered with soft carpeting.

Now, that alone was a rare and pleasurable feature worthy of anyone's eulogy. But in the wondrous eyes of a boy there was something else to make a visit long to be remembered. Yea, even unto forty years! For when seated there of a pleasant morning with the door slightly ajar, one could see through the honeysuckle a patch of blue sky and the white sails of four catboats, serenely sailing around a circular course above the ridge of the adjacent workshop.

Each boat in turn would luff up, bear away on the starboard tack, and eventually gybe over to port. All the evolutions of a real yacht in a race were there—the beat, the run and the reach. Childishly you wished one boat would overhaul and pass the one ahead, but somehow you knew danged well it never would. While you watched and dreamed, all else was forgotten, even your surroundings —well, almost.

There was a practical feature also. To be sure, the schooner model with its mainsail set, which veered atop the barn, gave the wind direction, but the catboat race showed the force. The faintest breath would start the boats moving, and when it was really blowing they would chase around so fast that any moment you expected to see a boat go sailing way off over Charlie Brown's garden next door.

The construction of this device was fairly simple and is easy to duplicate. Four identical 10 inch models were carved out of soft pine and neatly painted. The masts were of oak and securely stepped in position. The sails were cut from sheet zinc, painted white, and secured to the masts with brass straps in such a manner as to allow them to swing freely to port and to starboard. As shown in the diagram, the mainsheets were small brass chain, stapled to the deck with enough scope to permit the sails to swing off 30 to 40 degrees either way. The models were then mounted at each end of the crossbars, which were of oak about $\frac{1}{2}$ by $1\frac{1}{2}$ inches and 4 feet long. The whole assembly was then placed atop a short pole which was nailed to the gable, projecting above the ridge not over 2 feet. A simple bearing was provided for and well greased, as the less friction the more sensitive the device would be.

In operation it is obvious that, regardless of wind direction, at all times one sail is in the wind and the other three are working.

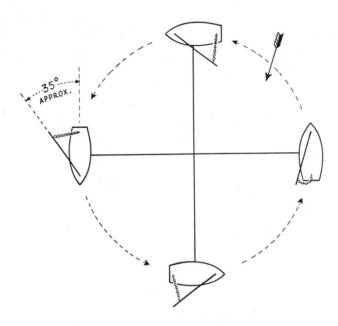

Making A Mast Boot

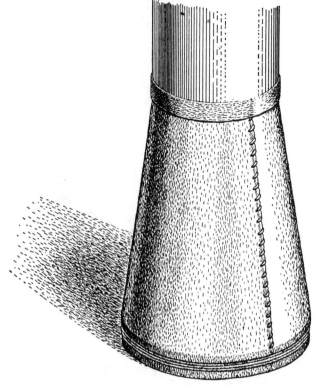

CONSIDERING the fact that the making of a simple mast boot involves nothing more than fitting a scrap of canvas about the mast at the deck to exclude water, it is surprising how often the result takes on the appearance of a too large garterless sock. On the other hand, a well designed boot has a tailored look so smooth and sleek that it never offends the eye. The mast seems to literally grow out of the deck.

A good mast boot should be absolutely watertight, good looking and permanent. By permanent I mean so designed that the mast can be unshipped without destroying the boot. The type shown here meets these requirements.

A wood collar, three-quarters by one inch, is made to fit the deck, keeping a quarter of an inch away from the mast hole in order to clear the mast wedges. This collar is made in two pieces for a round mast, four for a rectangular one. A quarter of an inch groove is cut all around the outside edge and is then bedded in white lead or bedding compound, and secured to the deck with brass screws.

The boot is a piece of twelve ounce canvas, cut as shown in the diagrams. Take your measurements accurately and make a paper pattern before cutting the

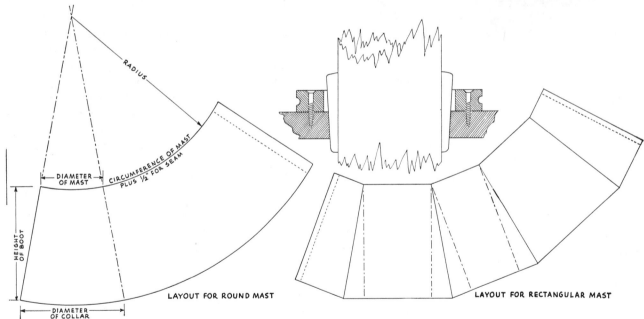

LAYOUT FOR ROUND MAST

LAYOUT FOR RECTANGULAR MAST

canvas. When satisfied that it fits exactly, place the boot about the mast, turn under the raw edges and sew it up, using doubled sail twine in a round seam. The seam should be on the after side of the mast.

Now slip it down the mast until it covers the collar. Take three or four turns about it with tarred hemp marline and secure, drawing it up tightly until the canvas is forced into the groove in the collar. Secure the

top of the boot to the mast with waterproof adhesive tape, at least four turns.

The boot should have two coats of deck paint, but knowing that nothing rots canvas quicker than linseed oil, a coat of shellac should first be applied.

At fall layup time cut the marline securing the boot to the collar and pull your mast with the boot attached. What could be simpler?

[107]

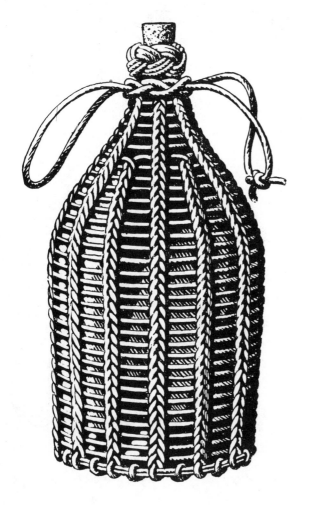

The Water Jug

certainly as though he carried a sign on his back I knew the boy's lineage, for only Capt. Van W. would have had the foresight and ability to do a job like that.

The jug shown here is covered with French hitching, which gives a ribbed effect somewhat like knitting. Tarred fishline is used, with a large sail needle to pass the hitches, starting at the bottom and working upward to the neck. Hold the jug upside down between your knees and pass two turns of line around it close to the bottom. Then start a series of loop-stitches or hitches as shown in the diagram.

After the first circuit continue by adding another row of hitches around those already worked. Keep an even tension throughout and the ribs lined up straight. When you have worked up over the shoulder of the jug to where it narrows into the neck, omit every other hitch and continue to the end with half the number of ribs.

To cover the bottom start a series of hitches around the turns first placed on the jug, between the ribs that cover the sides. Omit hitches at regular intervals as the diameter reduces, and secure all at the center.

Finish off the job with a 3 strand Turk's head around the neck. A jug sling knot tied in ¼ inch white cotton line is placed about the neck below the Turk's head to serve as a handle.

E VERY yachtsman knows the vital importance of fresh drinking water, and generally has some sort of portable container which he stows carefully in the dinghy before shoving off on a clamming expedition. It may be an old stone jug his great-grandfather used aboard the Fanny C, or just a 1947 model half gallon cider bottle from the corner chain store. Whatever its character, the marline spike sailor inevitably covers it neatly with hitching or netting as a protection from breakage.

Recently I saw a small boy trudging home from the creek, a sailbag slung over his shoulder and carrying with his free hand the biggest vacuum bottle I have ever seen, and it was covered with hitching, sailor fashion. As

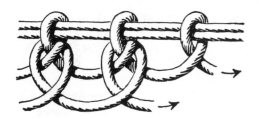

French hitching

The jug sling knot

[108]

Registration Numbers

They Too Can Be Beautiful

ALL yacht owners recognize the importance of proper registration of motor boats and auxiliaries. But the numbers themselves are generally considered to be a necessary evil insofar as appearance is concerned. Black numbers on a white hull can often interrupt the eye and break up a beautiful sheer line. In many cases the numbers actually mar the appearance of a yacht and give her a downright commercial look. Then there's the problem of repainting the numbers during the spring overhaul. Any way you look at it the numbers are a nuisance, be they ever so necessary.

With these thoughts in mind I humbly submit the suggestion here illustrated. It is an adaptation of the nameboards carried on the bows of the coasting schooners many years ago. (The word "adaptation" to an artist means lifted, swiped, stolen or copied line for line.) Actually it was taken from the nameboards of the schooner Louis V. Place, wrecked on Fire Island Beach opposite Sayville in 1895.

The beveled edges, carved ornaments and the numbers are gold-leafed. The background can be either the same color as the hull or, in some instances, a contrasting color. It all depends on the design of the hull, the type of rail or sheer strake, and the general color scheme. Do not use varnished mahogany with gold numbers—it results in poor legibility and defeats the purpose of the numbers, which is easy identification of the yacht.

The board should be made of a hard, close grained wood, well seasoned, and not over one-half inch thick. The numbers are incised, with a shallow vee-cut. When completed, give it a prime coat of thin paint followed by one of enamel undercoat. Use a high quality outside enamel for the background.

If you have had experience in applying gold-leaf no instructions need be given here. If not, you would be wise to let a sign painter do it for you, as it is a tricky piece of business. Secure the board to the hull with a couple of round head brass screws, and come next spring you can easily remove it. Better yet, put it on the mantel during the winter lay-up, right under the picture of Uncle Horace.

Carved dolphin tiller head

Art and Yacht Design

IT ALL started with Marvin's Livery Stable — must have been along about 1906 or thereabouts, for I was just a small boy making my first unescorted journey by train for a visit with my grandfather. The idea of traveling alone made it a momentous occasion, and as I stood on the station platform with my belongings (a nightshirt, pair of stockings and a jacknife) I was a very important person. Jimmy, the little hunchbacked stage driver, had been told to meet me, and as he took my bag asked, "You goin' to Cap'n Jim Berry's?" I nodded. "Thought so," he said. "Hop in and let's get goin'. Got to stop at the stable on the way, but I guess you ain't in no hurry."

Some fifteen minutes later we pulled up in front of the barn and stopped, and while Jimmy disappeared inside I sat transfixed. There above the open door of the stable, all aglitter in the morning sun, was an enormous golden eagle, its wings outstretched some twelve feet from tip to tip. It was the most wonderful thing I had ever seen, and although the details have faded with the years I still remember how fierce he looked, crouching with his head turned and talons extended. As Jimmy climbed back on the seat and gathered up the reins I begged him to tell me all about it, but all I could get from him was, "Aw, just some ole carvin' offen a ship."

Right then and there I made a solemn vow that some day I would own a ship with a golden eagle, the word "ship" being a boy's rather vague, all inclusive term covering everything from a rowboat to a square rigger.

Well, after some forty years of blood, sweat and tears I own a "ship" with an eagle, and although the "ship" is a little small to be so classified, the eagle glitters just as brightly, and inspires just as many daydreams as did the one on Marvin's Livery Stable so long ago.

All of which provides the soft organ music background for the subject matter of this chapter, traditional ornamentation and yacht design from the artist's view-

Traditional bronze star on plate, protecting end grain of bitts

Traditional treatment of boom end. Gold star in relief, white background and gold cove border

Typical clipper bow, showing carved and gilded head and incised scroll decorating the trail boards

point. Realizing that anything I say may be used against me, yet being prepared to stand the consequences, it is my considered opinion that yacht designers in general have for the past fifty years missed the boat. They have let us down. They have turned their backs on 300 years of tradition and experience in the creation of ships of beauty and given us faster more efficient sailing machines stripped of all decoration, modern as all get-out, and utterly devoid of the romance of the sea which should have been our heritage. Instead of a personalized figurehead we get a combination bowlight-anchorchock-flag-

staff. Instead of a raised quarterdeck with its broken sheer terminating in a beautiful carved beak we have a flush deck with a sheer of no character. From a beautifully ornamented stern which pulls at your heartstrings and sets you dreaming of far places we have degenerated to a shapeless expanse of near-mahogany, bearing the name "Rob-Mar-Ed" in gold decals.

It is not enough that a yacht should be weatherly, smart and efficient. She should be beautiful and appealing, not to the eye alone but to the heart as well, arousing envy in the beholder and bringing a bit of romance, of

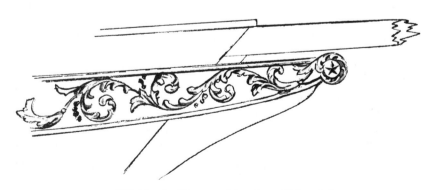

Billet head with more elaborate scroll in relief

[111]

Counter stern with applied carvings in color and gold

makebelieve to the owner. Once in a blue moon such a design does appear—with Romance written in invisible ink all over it. You see Spanish galleons, East Indiamen, privateers and Baltimore clippers . . . and you are a boy again. But the number of yacht designers able to turn out a beautiful boat can be counted on the fingers of one hand. They are men who are saturated with tradition and sea lore, insatiable researchers, and above all, consciously or not, artists at heart. And they have a hell of a lot of fun doing it.

I am not a naval architect and therefore would not presume to sound off as such. But as an artist with many years of yachting experience I have formed certain opinions and reached conclusions pertinent to the question. I believe it is possible to achieve the enchantment of the olden times with a modern hull. As I see it, we have three things to work with—line, color and form—but to put them all together takes imagination, an element which seems to be totally lacking in many designers. Basically I would like to see a return to the use of carving and ornamentation. It would have to be used intelligently, with a great amount of restraint and a high regard for, and a well versed knowledge of tradition.

Of course not all types of hulls lend themselves to decorative treatment. A figurehead on a Cape Cod cat

would look rather silly, and so would a carved eagle on a Star boat's transom. But on the other hand a Friendship sloop, Chesapeake bugeye or skipjack, and the hull with the true clipper bow and counter stern offer plenty of opportunity for embellishment. Because there has been a slight revival in recent years of clipper bow, and because the clipper bow is the most beautiful yacht form ever developed, I have made it the subject of the illustrations accompanying this article. Actually the subject of yacht ornamentation is too involved and comprehensive to cover adequately in the limits of this chapter, and the most I can do is to suggest a few of the possibilities as I see them.

The clipper bow is the most difficult of all forms to design. Howard Chapelle, in his *Yacht Designing and Planning* states, "The conventions of design that establish the correct appearance of the clipper bow were developed in early times, and these conventions are as absolute as those of the classical orders in architecture." While the forms varied in the interpretations of different designers the type is more or less static, and it does not take an expert to spot one that is poorly designed. Here is an opportunity to have a figurehead, and while there is a choice of subject the eagle is the most commonly used. The scroll carved in the trail boards is incised with a shallow vee cut and goldleafed. The design is kept simple because the size of the yacht is small. The alternate design features a carved billet head, which is entirely traditional, and the scroll is in relief and more elaborate. The larger the yacht, the more involved can be your decoration, and scale is of the utmost importance.

With the clipper bow goes the true counter stern. Here you can give your imagination full play, and research on old ships can give priceless inspiration. I might say that the traditional motifs most commonly used in American ships were the ribbon, the eagle, patriotic emblems, stars, dolphins, rope moldings, leaf forms, and the cornucopia or horn of plenty. Colors used were red, white, blue, gray, black, goldleaf, and sometimes green. Yellow was often used, particularly on moldings, but generally as a cheap substitute for gilding. I have shown two traditional treatments of the conventional counter stern, both featuring the inevitable eagle.

Stars have been prominent decorative motifs on ships ever since the creation of our national emblem, and rightly so. In the Navy gun-tampions have always borne a star. Boom ends often were carved with a star in relief, as I have shown. A brass or bronze plate with a raised star protects the head of a bitt from the weather.

Yachts steered by a tiller have always had carved tiller heads, much as I have shown, often with a carved fancy knot, eagle head or dragon.

These are but a few of the many ways in which ornamentation may be applied to yachts, and I feel that if more yachtsmen were familiar with the subject and aware of the infinite number of ways in which personality, character and romance can be attained, our yacht designers would stop playing with plastics and chrome plating and give us more eagles and goldleaf. They probably would not make much money, but we would have more fun.

Design for counter stern, showing use of carved and gilded rope molding

Synthetic Fibers
and Their Characteristics

POLYESTER

Polyester is more commonly known as DACRON, by DuPont, or FORTREL by Celanese Corporation. It is a long chain synthetic polyamide product from ethylene glycol and terephthalic acid, formed into a continuous filament.

Although dacron rope is nearly as strong as nylon, it has only half the elasticity. While nylon can lose about 10% of its strength when wet, dacron retains nearly its full strength and durability after immersion.

With a specific gravity of 1.38, dacron is heavier than nylon, and more expensive, but because of its excellent wet abrasion characteristics it can, if handled properly, give a service life as good or better than nylon.

Because of its low stretch and wearing qualities, it is univerally preferred for sheets and halyards. Available in either laid or braided construction, dacron rope is soft to the feel and easy on the hands. It has a high melting point of 480° F., is completely impervious to rot and mildew, and has good resistance to acids. Therefore it can be machine washed with a mild soap or detergent.

POLYPROPYLENE AND POLYETHYLENE

Polypropylene is a thermo-plastic resin from the polarization of propylene, a product of oil refining, then extruded and drawn, whereas polyethylene is a resin formed from the polarization of ethylene.

Both filaments are similar in nature, but in almost every instance, polypropylene is superior in performance. Both are very light in weight, with a specific gravity of .90 for polypropylene and .95 for polyethylene, and therefore will float indefinitely.

Both of these filaments are twice as strong as manila, but only half as strong as nylon and dacron. They have a very low melting point of 300° F., and begin to lose tensile

strength at a little over 200° F. Neither has a very good abrasion resistance nor the ability to absorb shock loads. The fibers tend to break down under ultraviolet light conditions, and should have adequate inhibitors. Therefore the rope is generally black or other dark colors.

Neither polypropylene nor polyethylene will absorb water and are resistant to most common acids and alkalis.

In the pleasure boating field these ropes are very popular with the uninformed, mainly because of their low initial cost and the variety of colors that can be obtained. To the better informed, this is foolish. Because of the variations in quality, both in filament and rope construction, plus the less desirable physical characteristics of these materials, it is a wiser investment both financially and safety-wise to buy a nylon or dacron rope.

Polypropylene may be used for short-time docking, but where the rope lays in a chock, the fibers can melt and fuse from friction under heavy intermittent loads.

Polyethylene rope is slippery and greasy to the feel, and when knots, bends or hitches are employed, they can slip or untie. Its use is confined mainly to ski-tow ropes.

There are available several ropes, both braided and 3-strand laid, employing a combination of nylon and polypropylene. These give much better abrasion resistance and higher strength than an all-polypropylene rope.

NYLON

Nylon is a long chain synthetic polyamide fiber derived from petroleum and natural gas products.

There are two types of nylon in common use today, with minor differences in physical characteristics. The best nylon rope is made of *continuous filament* nylon. *Spun* nylon has a fuzzy appearance and a softer feel, and is less strong.

Nylon is especially noted for its ability to absorb shock loads, its great elasticity, high tensile strength, and resistance to chafing and abrasion. Compared to manila, it is approximately the same weight and has 3 to 4 times the tensile strength. While the cost of nylon is approximately 2½ times that of manila rope, it will last 4 to 5 times longer. These unique characteristics of high strength and elasticity give it a very high margin of safety with less chance of breaking or cutting.

Nylon has a melting point of 440° F. It has a specific gravity of 1.14, and therefore sinks in water. It is highly resistant to alkalis, can be machine-washed with a small amount of soap or detergent, and is rotproof. It will absorb small amounts of water, and will shrink approximately 10% when wet.

Because of its great elasticity and strength, nylon rope is superb for anchor cables and mooring lines. It absorbs the shock of sudden surges like a rubber band, and is far easier on the boat and gear than the manila rope formerly used. It is made in both laid and braided construction, and in the latter is available with a polypropylene core . . . a very superior product.

Basic Eye Splice
for SAMSON 2-in-1 Braided Ropes

BACKGROUND INFORMATION

Samson Spliceable Braided Ropes have a braided CENTER rope inside a braided COVER rope — "a rope inside a rope". Therefore, when splicing, ALWAYS TIE A KNOT approximately 5 FID LENGTHS FROM THE END YOU ARE SPLICING. THIS KEEPS THE TWO "ROPES" LOCKED TOGETHER while splicing. (See Fid)

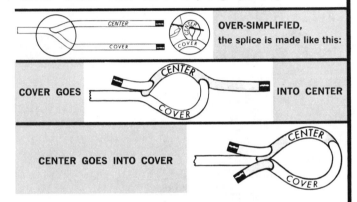

OVER-SIMPLIFIED, the splice is made like this:

COVER GOES **INTO CENTER**

CENTER GOES INTO COVER

SPLICING TOOLS

FID: A different sized fid is needed with each diameter of 2-in-1 Braided Line. Ex: ⅜" Line use ⅜" fid.

Fid used to guide the cover through the center rope and vice versa. Fid is also a measuring tool. Note scribe mark and short section.

PUSHER: This tool pushes the fid and cover through center rope and vice versa.

TAPE: One tight layer of tape should be wrapped on both ends of cover and center to keep strands from fraying. End can then be inserted into the fid.

MARKING PEN: Or soft lead pencil, grease crayon, ball point pen to mark measurements.

KNIFE OR SCISSORS

MEASURE THE EYE ◄ STEP 1

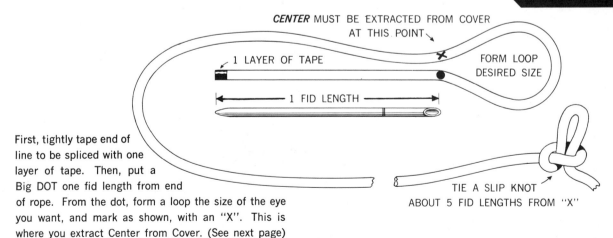

CENTER MUST BE EXTRACTED FROM COVER AT THIS POINT

1 LAYER OF TAPE

FORM LOOP DESIRED SIZE

1 FID LENGTH

TIE A SLIP KNOT ABOUT 5 FID LENGTHS FROM "X"

First, tightly tape end of line to be spliced with one layer of tape. Then, put a Big DOT one fid length from end of rope. From the dot, form a loop the size of the eye you want, and mark as shown, with an "X". This is where you extract Center from Cover. (See next page) Now tie knot about 5 fid lengths from X.

EXTRACT CENTER FROM COVER

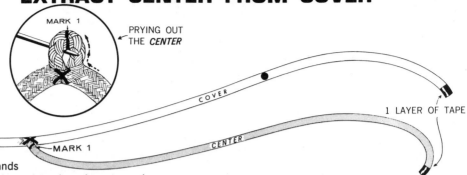

Bend the rope sharply at "X". Spread Cover strands apart firmly with the point of pusher, to make an opening, so you can pry out the Center (as seen in insert).

Mark **one** big line on the Center where it comes out. This is Mark #1.

Now, use your fingers to pull **all** the Center out of the Cover from "X" to the end, as above.

You'll notice a paper identification marker tape **inside** the center. Pull on tape until it breaks at knot. You want to get rid of it so you can do splice.

Put a single layer of tape on end of Center.

MARK THE CENTER ◀ STEP 3

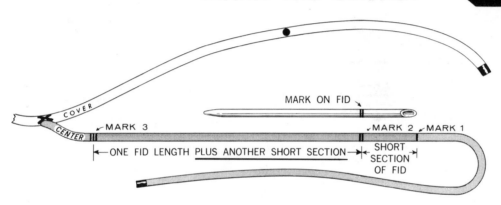

As shown, pull out more of the Center. From Mark #1, measure a distance equal to the **short section** of the fid. Mark **two** heavy lines. This is Mark #2. Now, mark **three** heavy lines at a distance one fid length **plus** one short section of fid from Mark #2. Call this Mark #3. Compare your marks with picture above.

PUSH FID THROUGH CENTER "TUNNEL"

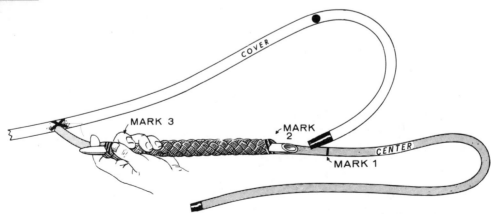

Using a thimble? See "Tips" on Back Cover.
Insert fid into Center at Mark #2. Slide fid lengthwise thru "tunnel" from Mark #2 until the point sticks out at Mark #3 as shown.

[118]

NOW, PUSH COVER THRU CENTER TUNNEL ◄ STEP 5

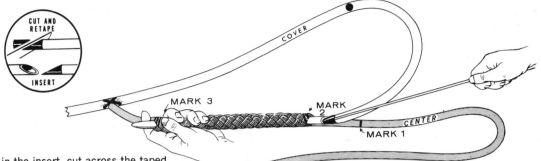

As in the insert, cut across the taped end of the Cover to form a point. Retape tightly with **one layer of tape** to make the point firm. Now, jam the taped point of the cover into the open end of the fid.

Next, jam the pusher into the fid behind the tape.

Holding the Center **gently** at Mark #3, push both fid and cover through the "tunnel" from Mark #2 to Mark #3, until the Dot almost disappears into center at Mark #2. Leave the cover tail sticking out and turn to the next page.

STEP 6 ► PUSH CENTER TAIL THRU COVER

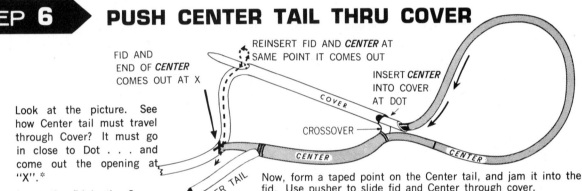

Look at the picture. See how Center tail must travel through Cover? It must go in close to Dot . . . and come out the opening at "X".*

Insert the fid in the Cover, at your original dot. This is the "Crossover". Slide fid through the "tunnel", pointing towards "X". If it reaches "X", fine. If not, push the point through the cover strands, as in picture, for later reinsertion.*

Now, form a taped point on the Center tail, and jam it into the fid. Use pusher to slide fid and Center through cover.

After fid comes out at "X", continue to pull **all** Center tail through the "tunnel". Pull it tight.

Now go back to **Cover** tail and pull **it** tight, too, so crossover is tight in both directions.

*NOTE: One pass is enough for small eye. On large eyes several passes may be necessary for the fid to reach the "X". When this occurs simply reinsert fid at exact place it comes out, and continue to "X".

TAPER THE END OF THE COVER ◄ STEP 7

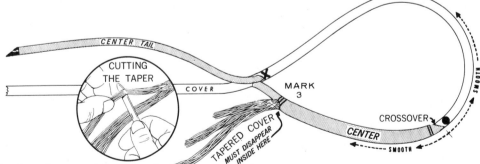

Cut off taped section from the cover tail. Unravel the cover tail braid (see insert) all the way to where it comes out of center of Mark #3. Cut off groups of strands at **staggered** intervals, as shown, to form a tapered end.

Now hold the loop in one hand at the crossover. Firmly smooth both sides of the loop away from crossover. Do this until the tapered cover tail section completely disappears inside Mark #3.

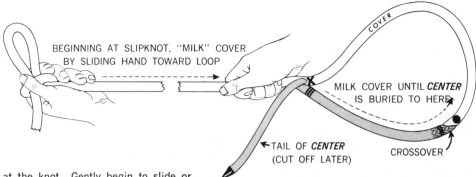

BEGINNING AT SLIPKNOT, "MILK" COVER
BY SLIDING HAND TOWARD LOOP

COVER

MILK COVER UNTIL *CENTER*
IS BURIED TO HERE

◄ TAIL OF *CENTER*
(CUT OFF LATER)

CROSSOVER

Next hold rope at the knot. Gently begin to slide or "milk" the Cover slack toward the loop. You'll now see the Center begin to disappear or "bury" in the Cover. Go back to the knot, and continue milking more and more firmly until all Center **and** the Crossover are buried inside the Cover.

IF BURYING GETS DIFFICULT . . . Sometimes bunching occurs at Crossover. This may hinder burying. So, tug firmly on tail of Center, until bunching disappears. Then, resmooth loop as in Step #7. Continue burying until Crossover is buried completely. Sometimes you can make burying easier by flexing the buried section up to the crossover.

FINALLY, CUT OFF THE CENTER TAIL. After burying is completed, firmly smooth the finished eye in the direction of the tail. Then cut off the center tail "fairly close" to the cover. The cut end should just **barely** disappear at X, when you tug at the top of the eye.

FINISHING OFF. Eye Splice should look as in picture. We recommend simple whipping of the eye splice near throat.

If a "hollow" spot appears at the throat, **don't worry.** You merely cut core tail too close, before it slipped into the Cover. (For the sake of neatness, you may want to adjust on your next splice.) However, the hollow spot does NOT affect splice performance or strength: Total load of an eye splice is SHARED between its own two legs. Each leg, therefore, supports 50% of the load. Naturally, the Braided Cover **alone** can handle this load.

Standard End-for-End

The Samson Standard End-for-End Splice can be performed on new and used rope. This is an all-purpose splice technique designed for people who generally splice used rope as frequently as new rope. It retains up to 85% of average new rope strength and in used rope up to 85% of the remaining used rope strength.

STEP 1 . . . MAKING THE MEASUREMENTS

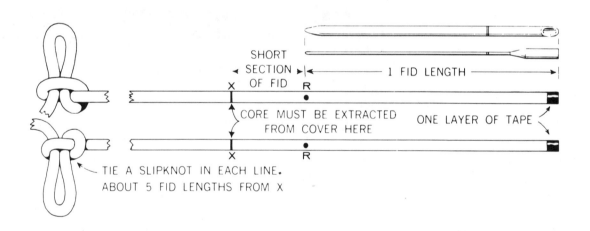

SHORT
SECTION
OF FID

1 FID LENGTH

CORE MUST BE EXTRACTED
FROM COVER HERE

ONE LAYER OF TAPE

TIE A SLIPKNOT IN EACH LINE.
ABOUT 5 FID LENGTHS FROM X

Tape the end of each rope with one thin layer of tape. Lay two ropes to be spliced side by side and measure one fid length from end of each rope and make a mark. This is Point R (Reference).

From R measure one short fid section length as scribed on the fid; then, mark again. This is Point X where you should extract core from inside cover. Be sure both ropes are identically marked.

Tie a tight slipknot approximately 5 fid lengths from X.

STEP 2 . . . EXTRACTING THE CORES

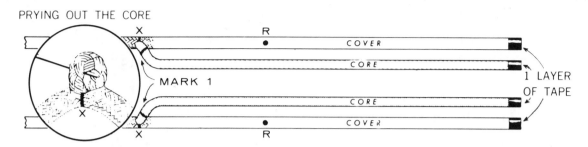

PRYING OUT THE CORE

Bend rope sharply at X. With the pusher or any sharp tool such as an ice pick, awl, or marlin spike, spread cover strands to expose core. First pry; then, pull core completely out of cover from X to the end of rope. Put one layer only of tape on end of core.

To assure correct positioning of Mark #1 do the following.

Holding the exposed core, slide cover as far back towards the tightly tied slip knot as you can. Then, firmly smooth cover back from the slip knot towards taped end. Smooth again until all cover slack is removed. Then, mark core where it comes out of cover. This is Mark #1. Do this to both ropes.

MARKING THE CORES . . . STEP 3

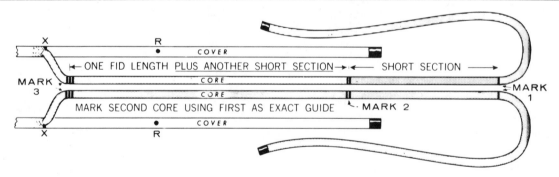

Hold one core at Mark #1 and slide cover back to expose more core.

From Mark #1, measure along core towards X a distance equal to the short section of fid and make two heavy marks. This is Mark #2.

From Mark #2, measure in the same direction *one fid length plus another short section* and make three heavy marks. This is Mark #3.

Mark second core by laying it alongside the first and using it as an exact guide.

MARKING THE COVERS FOR TAPERING . . . STEP 4

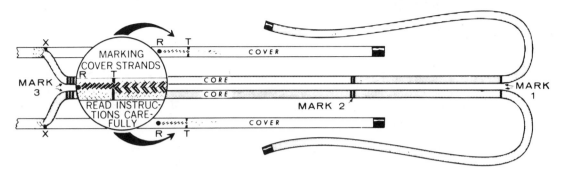

Note nature of the cover braid. It is made up of strand pairs. By inspection you can see that half the pairs revolve to the right around the rope and half revolve to the left.

Beginning at R and working toward the taped end of cover, count 7 consecutive pairs of cover strands which revolve to the right (or left). Mark the 7th pair. This is Point T (See Insert). Make Mark T go completely around cover.

Starting at T and working toward taped cover end *count* and *mark every second right pair* of strands for a total of 6. Again, starting at T, count and mark every second left pair of strands for a total of 6. (See Insert).

Make both ropes identical.

STEP 5 . . . PERFORMING THE TAPER

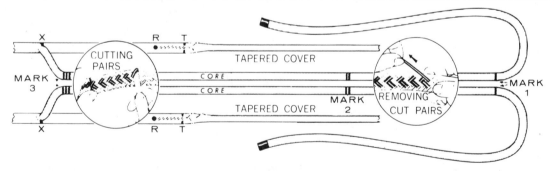

First remove tape from cover end. Starting with last marked pair of cover strands toward the end, cut and pull them completely out (See Insert). Cut and remove next marked strands and continue with each right and left marked strands until you reach Point T. *Do not cut beyond this point.* (See Insert)

Retape tapered end.

Cut and remove marked strands on the other marked cover, again stopping at T. Retape tapered end.

STEP **6** . . . REPOSITIONING THE ROPES

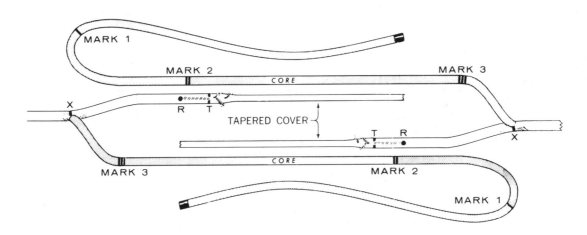

Reposition ropes for splicing according to diagram. Note how cover of one rope has been paired off with core of the opposite line. *Avoid twisting.*

PUTTING THE COVER INSIDE CORE . . . STEP **7**

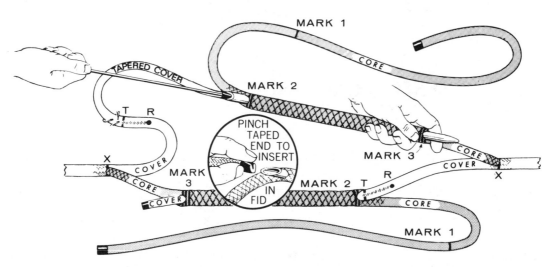

Insert fid into one core at Mark #2 and bring it out at Mark #3. Add extra tape to tapered cover end then jam it tightly into hollow end of fid (see insert). Hold core lightly at Mark #3, place pusher point into taped end pushing fid and with cover in it from Mark #2 out at· Mark #3. When using metal fids for larger rope, screw fid onto taped cover. Pull fid through from Mark #2 to Mark #3. Don't screw cover into fid as twists will develop in line. Pull cover tail through core until Mark T on cover meets Mark #2 on core. Insert other cover into core in same manner.

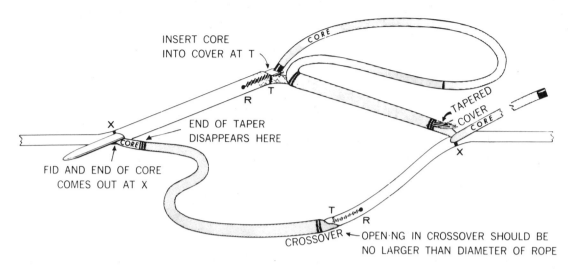

Now put core back into cover from T to X. Insert fid at T, jam taped core tightly into end of fid. With pusher, push fid and core through cover bringing out at Point X. When using metal fid screw fid onto taped core — not visa-versa. Then pull fid and braid through from T to X. Do this to both cores. Remove tape from end of cover. Bring crossover up tight by pulling on core tail and on tapered covered tail. Hold crossover tightly smoothing out all excess braid away from crossover in each direction. Tapered cover tail will disappear at Mark #3. Cut core tail off close to Point X.

STEP 9 . . . BURYING THE EXPOSED CORE

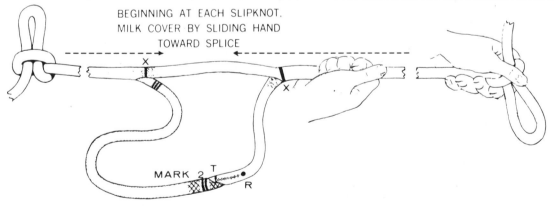

Hold rope at slipknot and with other hand milk cover toward the splice, gently at first, and then more firmly. The cover will slide over Mark #3, Mark #2 the crossover and R. Repeat with the other side of the splice.

Continue burying until *all cover slack between the knot and the splice* has been removed.

STEP 10. . . FINISHING THE SPLICE

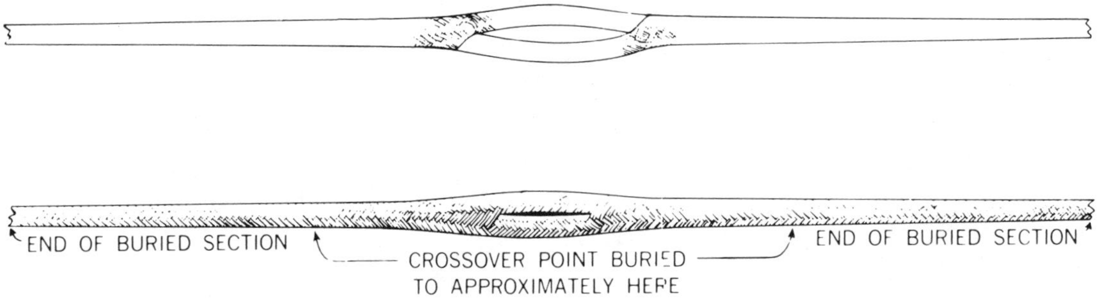
END OF BURIED SECTION
CROSSOVER POINT BURIED
TO APPROXIMATELY HERE
END OF BURIED SECTION

The splice is done when *all* cover slack has been removed and there is an opening in the splice approximately equal in length to the diameter of rope. If at the opening one side of the splice is noticeably longer than the other side, something is wrong. Check Steps 1-9 and remake if necessary.

Now untie the slip knots.

★

Back Splice

The Samson Back Splice is a neat and permanent way to terminate the end of a line. It is flexible and can be tapered to reduce bulk. To make a Back Splice half as long as described, use half measurements.

MAKING THE MEASUREMENTS . . . STEP 1

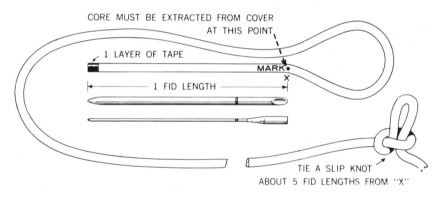

Tape end to be spliced with one thin layer of tape. Then, measure one fid length from end of rope and mark. This is Point X (Extraction).

Tie a tight slip knot approximately five fid lengths from X. *This must be done.*

STEP **2** . . . **EXTRACTING THE CORE**

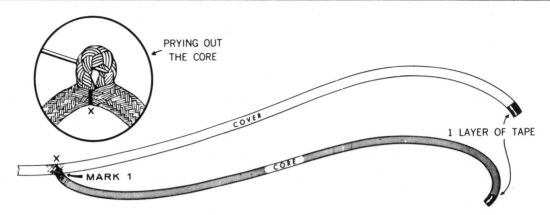

PRYING OUT THE CORE

COVER

1 LAYER OF TAPE

CORE

X

MARK 1

Bend rope sharply at X. With pusher or any sharp tool such as an ice pick, awl, or marlin spike, separate cover strands to expose core. First pry; then, pull core completely out of cover from X to the rope end. Put one layer only of tape on end of core.

To assure *correct* positioning of Mark #1 do the following.

Holding exposed core, slide the cover as far back towards the tightly tied slip knot as you can. Then, firmly smooth cover back from slip knot towards the taped end. Smooth again until all cover slack is removed. Then, mark core where it comes out of the cover. This is Mark #1.

STEP **3** . . . **MARKING THE CORE**

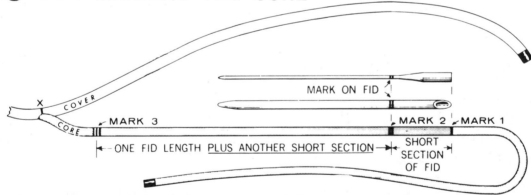

MARK ON FID

X

COVER

CORE

MARK 3

MARK 2

MARK 1

ONE FID LENGTH PLUS ANOTHER SHORT SECTION

SHORT SECTION OF FID

Again slide cover towards the slipknot to expose more core.

From Mark #1 measure along core towards X a distance equal to the *short section* of fid and make two heavy marks. This is Mark #2.

From Mark #2 measure in the same direction *one fid length plus another short section* of the fid and make 3 heavy marks. This is Mark #3.

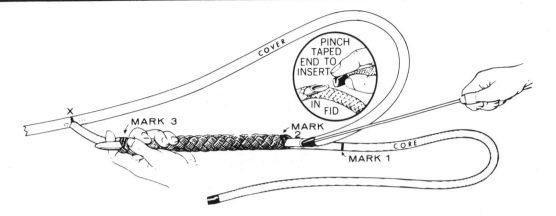

Insert fid into core at Mark #2. Slide fid through and out at Mark #3.

Pinch taped end of cover, jam it tightly into hollow end of fid (See Insert). Hold core lightly at Mark #3, place the pusher point into the taped end, and push fid and cover through from Mark #2 and out at Mark #3. When using metal fids for larger size ropes screw fid on to taped cover. *Don't* try to screw cover into fid as this will produce twists in the line. After fid is on, milk the braid over the fid while pulling fid through from Mark #2 to Mark #3.

ADJUSTING THE CORE OVER COVER . . . STEP 5

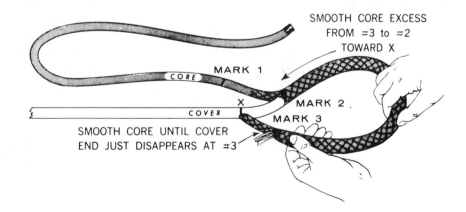

Remove tape from cover end. Smooth core from Mark #2 towards Mark #3 until cover ends *just* disappear inside.

Next, holding core at Mark #3, smooth core from Mark #3 to Mark #2. Do this until all excess is eliminated.

STEP **6** . . . BURYING THE EXPOSED CORE

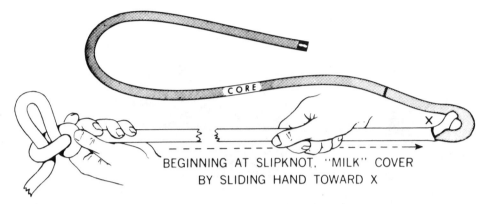

BEGINNING AT SLIPKNOT, "MILK" COVER
BY SLIDING HAND TOWARD X

Hold rope at slipknot and with other hand, milk the cover toward splice, gently at first, and then more firmly. The cover will slide over Mark #3, Mark #2, and finally X. Be sure all excess cover is milked out so that X (a bump) is well inside the cover.

If final burying is difficult, flex the splice to loosen the strands, then continue burying.

STEP **7** . . . FINISHED SPLICE

CUT CORE END
OFF CLOSE

↙ END OF BURIED SECTION

Cut the protruding core off close at the cover. Once again milk cover towards the end so that it covers the cut off core.

Index

Abaca plant, 1

Baggywrinkle, 50, 51
Bell lanyard, 31, 35,
Bell pull, 39, 53, 59, 60
Bell rope, 87, 88
Berry, Capt. James H., 41
Bitt protection, 110
Blocks, vi, 2, 93, 94, 100, 101
Bilge pumps, wooden, 79, 80
Boltrope, vi
Boom end, 110
Bowline, 3, 4
Bucket rope, 35

Cannon lanyard, 102, 103
Canvas bucket, 95
Canvas sewing, 81, 82
Carrick bend, 4, 5, 39
Catboat model race, 105, 106
Chafing, 25, 26
Chafing gear, 50
Chapelle, Howard 112
Chest becket, 53
Chocks, 2
Cleats, metal 2
Cleats, wooden, 89, 90
Coachwipping, 58–60
Cockscombing, 64, 65
Constrictor knot, 37, 38
Counter stern, 112, 113
Crosby, Capt. Thomas L. 27, 67, 75
Cuprinol B. C. Green, 2

Deadeyes vi, 70–72
Diamond knot, 103
Ditty box, 75, 83
Door handle, 57
Double Becket hitch, 5
Drawer pull, 57

Fender, 21, 91, 92
Flemish coil, 41
Fungus, 2

Grafting, 61–63
Grommet, 15, 16

Haff, Hank, 41
Haight, Robert, 79
Hambroline, 23
Handles, rope 57
Harpoon, 5

Heaving line, 19–21
Henrietta, 41
Hitching
    French 108
    French spiral, 64
    needle, 61–63
    ringbolt, 64, 65
    Spanish, 61

Jackline, 97, 98
Jib, 97, 98
Josephine knot, 39

Kinks, 2
Knife handle, 59, 60
Knight's Modern Seamanship, 101

Ladder, Jacob's, 49
Ladder, rope 49, 50
Lanyard knot, 37, 38, 39
Lanyards, 53, 70–72
Lever, D'arcy, 39
Long splice, 11

Napoleon knot, 39, 41, 42
Numbers, 109
Nylon, 115

Magnus hitch, 5
Mast boat, 107
Mat
    block, 44
    ladder, 43
    rope 41, 42
    Russian, 45
    sword, 47
    walled, 45
Match hook, 22, 23
Mats, vi
Matthew Walker knot, 37, 39
Merriman snap hook, 98
Monkey's fist, 19, 20
Morning Star, 92
Mousing, 22, 23

Parceling 25, 26
Pointing, 61–63
Polyester, 115
Polyethylene, 116

Ratlines 22–24
Rolling hitch, 5
Rope v, vi, 1, 2
rope, coiling, 13

Rope construction, v
Rope, stowage 12, 13
Running splice, 11

Sails, v
    Cotton duck
    Synthetic
Sail stop bag, 99
Samson Cordage, v
Sea bag, 85
Sea chest, 67
Sea chest becket, 31, 35, 68
Seizing, vi, 22–24, 38
Sennit
    crown, 55, 56
    Nelson, 55, 56
    plaited, 52–54
Serving, 25, 66
Serving mallet, 25–27
Sheepshank, 3
Sheepskin, 51
The Sheet Anchor, 39
Sheet bend, 4
Short splice, 8, 9
Shrouds, rattled down, 22, 24
Slipped reef knot, 13
Splice, back
    synthetic braid, 127–30
Splice, end for end
    Synthetic braid, 121–26
Splice, eye
    hemp, 6, 7, 26
    synthetic braid, vi, 117–20
Splice, long, 11
Splice, short 8, 9
Star knot, 31–33
Stopper knot, 37

Tack knot, 35, 36
Tackle, 100, 101
Tiller head, 110, 113
Toggle and becket, 12–14
Tool bucket, 77, 78
Tool handle, 61
Turk's head, 28, 29

Wall knot, 37
Wall bag, 73, 74
Water jug, 63, 108
Whippings 17, 18
Worming 25

Yacht Designing and Planning, 112